Balance a Life

Happy **Life**

13 Weeks to Creating a Happier You

Elizabeth Gavino

BALBOA.
PRESS

A DIVISION OF HAY HOUSE

Balboa Press books may be ordered through booksellers or by contacting:

Balboa Press
A Division of Hay House
1663 Liberty Drive
Bloomington, IN 47403
www.balboapress.com
1 (877) 407-4847

Because of the dynamic nature of the Internet, any web addresses or links contained in this book may have changed since publication and may no longer be valid. The views expressed in this work are solely those of the author and do not necessarily reflect the views of the publisher, and the publisher hereby disclaims any responsibility for them.

The author of this book does not dispense medical advice or prescribe the use of any technique as a form of treatment for physical, emotional, or medical problems without the advice of a physician, either directly or indirectly. The intent of the author is only to offer information of a general nature to help you in your quest for emotional and spiritual well-being. In the event you use any of the information in this book for yourself, which is your constitutional right, the author and the publisher assume no responsibility for your actions.

Any people depicted in stock imagery provided by Thinkstock are models, and such images are being used for illustrative purposes only. Certain stock imagery © Thinkstock.

Print information available on the last page.

ISBN: 978-1-5043-3138-8 (sc)
ISBN: 978-1-5043-3140-1 (hc)
ISBN: 978-1-5043-3139-5 (e)

Library of Congress Control Number: 2015906076

Balboa Press rev. date: 04/27/2015

To lost love – without you my life would have taken a different path.

Contents

Part I
Soul-Nourishing Foods

Part II
13 Weeks to Balance and Happiness

Part III

Forward

By Tatiana Barrera, CHHC, Author of *No Milk Please*, and *No Mas a La Leche*

Elizabeth Gavino is to me much more than a peer author and health coach. Sharing a passion for healthy and enlightened living, Elizabeth and I have been good friends for years. Her giving personality and the high value she gives to friendship taught me more about the importance of feeding the soul for a healthy life than all the training I have received and the books I have read.

The book you have in your hands is a present, either from someone else, or from yourself; open your heart and receive it as the gift it is. Inside these pages you will find yourself traveling to the inside of your soul, and discovering untapped aspects of your own life and emotional health. As you read through it, you will open old doors and shine a new light on past experiences and lingering feelings.

As Elizabeth said to me in one of our long conversations, "I wear my heart on my sleeve." She is an open book, and the way she shares her own real life experiences will serve as a fascinating way to look into your past and connect with the lessons it has left you. Her honest and uplifting words come backed by a wealth of knowledge and an unparalleled tone of reality.

The messages, the exercises, and the journal in this book will make for a life-changing 13 week adventure, but it doesn't stop there. Get a copy for your night table, one for your living room, and one to keep at work. When in need of a word from a friend, open up Elizabeth's book, and re-read a chapter, or just a couple of pages, allowing your soul to indulge in the kind of food it may be craving.

Each of us has a different story, and each story can be read in countless different ways. The tools in this book will help you understand yours and turn it into a propeller to the future instead of a weight from the past.

Elizabeth is an expert in Soul-Nourishing Foods™, not only as an eager reader and researcher, but as one who has lived, and personally experienced their benefits. She is sharing with us powerful tools and strategies to live better.

Once you start implementing Elizabeth's recommendations, you will start to experience the kind of balance that promotes health and fulfillment. I have written about this balance from a perspective of alkalinity. The concept of alkalinity comes from the very chemical definition of the way our body functions at a cellular level. That delicate balance affects every function in our system. A body that maintains an alkaline balance is in a better position to regenerate, heal itself, and prevent disease and decay. And the opposite is also true. A body that is highly acidic is vulnerable to illness and accelerated aging, physical, mental and emotional.

You may have heard of the Alkaline Diet® and other nutritional theories that talk about alkalinity. They focus on the consumption of foods that are rich in water, oxygen and alkalizing minerals. These theories warn about acidifying foods like sugars, alcohol, caffeine and highly processed foods. I have studied, followed and recommended these principles for years. But it is not food alone that is responsible for attaining that healthy balance I call an Alkaline Lifestyle. Exercise, positive emotions, and stable relations are also key to maintaining balance and promoting a healthy environment in the body. There is no point in talking about alkaline foods alone, without considering these other important factors that affect our health.

Many times we hear of people who have tried countless diets with no luck. This frustrating yet common situation happens in part because not every diet is for everybody, but also because diet alone is never good enough. Even if you are on track with the proper nutrition for you, healthy eating is only one player in the team of elements that contributes to optimal health. Elizabeth's Soul-Nourishing Foods® are an excellent compilation of those other players in this game. Her book not only reminds you of their importance, but offers you actionable tools to work them and reap their benefits.

Confident that you will enjoy and benefit from Elizabeth's words as much as I have, I invite you to keep reading, and enjoy the journey.

It is a genuine honor and privilege for me to introduce you to a woman who will touch your heart and connect with you as only a real friend can do.

Preface

If you are reading this, know that I am you. I go through the same highs and lows that you go through. Commenting on the universality of human experience, my father always told me, "Know yourself; know the world." You are not alone in your feelings, and I hope knowing this brings you great comfort. Life is a journey and not an easy one, but I hope that through sharing my experiences, I can make the trip for you a little smoother and more fulfilling.

I had been "hungry" all my life. It was not a physical hunger, but rather a hunger within my soul for joy, peace, and a sense of completion. As I struggled to satiate that hunger, I was faced with many challenges. I suffered from an autoimmune disease which went undiagnosed until I was thirty-eight years old. Until that diagnosis, I had been prescribed unnecessary medications and suffered from malnutrition and mood swings. My health challenges were exacerbated by improper diet and a lack of balance in my approach to life. Business and other people's needs took precedence over my own.

I am a huge believer that everything happens for a reason. When I began writing this book, I was going through one of the greatest heartbreaks of my life. I was grieving for the love that I had lost and for the dreams that I had imagined for that relationship. I came to realize the experience, however difficult and painful, was absolutely necessary for me to undergo in order to bring you the wisdom and knowledge that I learned and continue to learn for myself. As I struggled to find my higher purpose and my life's meaning, I discovered my true self. As a result of this discovery, many of my health challenges have been overcome and I learned the importance of balance in my life. My hope is that through my story and experiences, you too, will come to find the inner peace and joy I am finally experiencing.

"Just when the caterpillar thought the world was
over, it became a butterfly" -Anonymous

Acknowledgements

*T*hose I Need to Thank

Never in my wildest imagination did I think I would become an author. It is my firm belief that people come into your life at various times for specific reasons.

Eric, you were meant to come into my life in order for this book to be conceived. Thank you for sending me the first message that brought us together. Without our time together, I would not have been forced to learn the lessons I needed for my growth and happiness.

If you are surrounded by a loving and supportive family as I am, then you, too, are wealthy.

To my parents, Barbara and Joe, you are my rock and my compass. Thank you for giving me a strong foundation that continues to guide me through life.

To my sister, Tania, Thank you for advising me to enroll in nutrition school. Your advice changed the course of my life forever.

To my niece, Kat, thank you for coming up with the brilliant book title. As you reminded me, sometimes you have to see life through the lens of a child. You are brilliant beyond your years.

To my nephew, Andres, I enjoyed bouncing ideas for my book with you. Always remember to walk along your own path to your dreams. You have many talents and I look forward to your creations.

There are those special people who come into your life whom you love as if they were family. These people are part of my tribe.

Patty, my sister from another mother and my best friend. Thank you for all the hours you spent listening to me and helping me through the highs and the lows in my life. I am blessed by our long and unyielding friendship.

Colette Austin, my editor and my teacher who set me on my initial course of writing, thank you for taking this journey with me. It has been wonderful collaborating with you. I hope we can work on many other future projects.

Tatiana Barrera, my friend and peer coach, I am so happy to have made the journey with you. Thank you for your mentorship and friendship.

Robin Kappy, thank you for your endless supply of wisdom that has helped me work through various aspects of my life.

Noorindah Iskandar, it was just a few years ago that we sat at the little French café and dreamt of where creativity and life would take us. Thank you for creating the beautiful book cover and celebrating my dreams with me.

To the countless others who have blessed me with their support, love, and friendship. A big THANK YOU for without you, I would be a different woman. I am grateful every day for each and every one of my family and friends who enrich my life and broaden my heart.

"When we become more fully aware that our success is due in large measure to the loyalty, helpfulness, and encouragement we have received from others, our desire grows to pass on similar gifts. Gratitude spurs us on to prove ourselves worthy of what others have done for us. The spirit of gratitude is a powerful energizer." — *Wilferd A. Peterson*

How to Use This Book

In my quest to find a balanced life, I have learned that we live in a society that expects everything to be fast - fast food, fast cars, fast answers, and fast weight loss. Expecting immediate results may not result in a lifelong change. As a consequence, we find ourselves on a hamster wheel continuously dieting, searching for happiness externally, and perpetuating the cycle of an unhappy and unfulfilled life.

There are three parts to this book. Part I provides a description of each Soul-Nourishing Food. Part II is the 13-week practice to strengthening each Soul-Nourishing Food. Finally, in Part III, you will find the Balanced Life, Happy Life Design Your Life Blueprint, the Balanced Life, Happy Life Journal, and the Financial Freedom Journal.

Part I: Understanding Soul-Nourishing Foods

In Part I, each chapter discusses a particular Soul-Nourishing Food and offers suggestions to help you work on that particular area.

In order to obtain the results you want, you need to understand and balance each of the 13 types of Soul-Nourishing Foods:

- Self-Care/Inner Joy
- Socialization
- Relationships
- Spirituality
- Career
- Money
- Enlightenment
- Home

- Creativity
- Health
- Movement
- Home Cuisine
- Dual Energies

Part II: Complete the 13-Week Practice

In Part II, you will learn how to implement various steps and ideas towards bettering a particular Soul-Nourishing Food. There are four 13-week cycles. Each week of the 13-week cycle, you will work on a particular Soul-Nourishing Food. By the end of the cycle, you should see improvement in each area. For best results, repeat the cycle three more times until the year has been completed. Feel free to continue working on your Soul-Nourishing Foods™ for as long as you would like and need to. Remember that this is a continual lifelong practice.

Part III: Record Your Goals, Emotions, and Finances

In Part III, you can begin journaling feelings and changes that you are experiencing or noticing. The act of journaling is a chance to think about what you want to change but to also acknowledge all the great things which are going well in your life. Too often, we spend more time focusing on the negatives in our lives rather than on the positives. It is in the acknowledgement of the little daily wins we each have that produce the greatest joy. The act of writing down your goals, feelings, and gratitude helps to shift your mental state. This is an important part of the process and should not be skipped. Make it a part of your morning of evening ritual to release all the chatter in your brain and to give you better perspective.

In the Financial Freedom Journal, you will be able to figure out your financial budgets in order to better reach your financial dreams and freedom. Change only occurs when we are aware of our spending.

Go to www.tastingwellness.com to sign up for bonus content. It is our way of thanking you for taking this journey to a balanced and happy life.

PART I
Soul-Nourishing Foods

Soul-Nourishing Foods™

What Are They?

There are many types of relationships – the relationship we have with ourselves, our loved ones, our career, our spirituality, our creativity, and even with our money. These "relationships" are what I call Soul-Nourishing Foods. Soul-Nourishing Foods are just as the name describes – foods that nourish the soul. They are areas in our lives that when in balance, feed our souls, make us happy and bring us serenity. When those areas are not fully developed, we find ourselves unhappy, unfulfilled and experiencing frequent malaise.

There are thirteen Soul-Nourishing Foods™:

- Self-Care/Inner Joy
- Socialization
- Relationships
- Spirituality
- Career
- Money
- Enlightenment
- Home
- Creativity
- Health
- Movement

- Home Cuisine
- Dual Energies

Physical food is what we eat for nutrition. Too often we eat food not because we are hungry but rather because one or more of the thirteen Soul-Nourishing Foods™ are out of balance. For example, someone who is having difficulty in a relationship with a partner will become stressed, sad, or anxious. They may have difficulty expressing their feelings for fear of further damaging the relationship. In an effort to avoid those feelings of stress, dread, or anxiety, they may turn to food for comfort and for avoidance.

Developing a specific Soul-Nourishing Food requires a little bit of patience, some time for exploration and contemplation, and practice. With the improvement and strengthening of each of the Soul-Nourishing Foods™, you will begin to see a shift in your health and emotional state.

> *"Recognize that when you are in balance, you possess a level of strength and flexibility that allows you to meet any challenge effortlessly." – Deepak Chopra*

As mentioned, food is not the only thing that can affect health. Disease is a symptom of life out of balance. Sometimes we carry hidden emotions that are locked up in our hearts. Years later they may manifest themselves in various medical conditions such as hypertension or heart conditions. This happened to Annemarie Colbin, founder of the Natural Gourmet Cooking School in New York City, and someone who ate mostly vegan and organic for years. One day, Annemarie was diagnosed with hypertension which came as a shock to her. She had read about the work of Dr. Samuel J. Mann, Professor of Clinical Medicine at the Hypertension Center of New York Presbyterian Hospital/Weill Cornell Medical Center. Over many years, Dr. Mann had seen thousands of patients with hypertension. He did not believe that his patient's hypertension arose from stress. Rather, he noticed that hypertension often resulted from repressed traumas. He wrote, "Even patients with severe hypertension did not seem more emotionally distressed than others. If anything, they seemed less distressed." [1] Annemarie knew that she needed to enact change in dealing with episodes of extreme high blood pressure. After some contemplation, she realized that the hypertension stemmed from childhood trauma that had not yet been resolved. After a few months of facing those memories and releasing emotions, she began to see her blood pressure improve until it eventually stabilized at a normal level.

The concept that our unbalanced life can bring about disease or conversely that a balanced life can bring about great health is an incredible testament to the power of the human body. This was the case for Annemarie Colbin as it is for me. The idea for this book came to me while I was in the middle of my nutrition course through the Institute for Integrative Nutrition. I had just broken up with the man I was in love with and was devastated by the loss of all the dreams I had envisioned for us. I was also in the midst of a changing industry for my primary profession, and I was in the middle of my nutrition program wondering what I was to do after the program was over. Additionally, I was dealing with lingering physical symptoms that traditional medical doctors could not remedy. I decided to consult a Naturopathic doctor. But something magical happened during this journey. I realized that both nutrition and external forces can affect our health. While proper physical nutrition nourishes our bodies, Soul-Nourishing Foods are just as important for every human being to feel balanced and to achieve optimal health. When one or more of these areas are off, we become unbalanced and seek other things to fill the void. These other things can be vices such as overeating unhealthy foods, drinking, shopping, smoking, and/or doing drugs which result from feeling stressed, lonely, angry, or sad. Stress in these areas can lead directly or indirectly to diseases such as cancer, depression, or to obesity. According to www.cancer.gov,

"The body responds to physical, mental, or emotional pressure by releasing stress hormones (such as epinephrine and norepinephrine) that increase blood pressure, speed heart rate, and raise blood sugar levels. These changes help a person act with greater strength and speed to escape a perceived threat.

Research has shown that people who experience intense and long-term (i.e., chronic) stress can have digestive problems, fertility problems, urinary problems, and a weakened immune system. People who experience chronic stress are

also more prone to viral infections such as the flu or common cold and to have
headaches, sleep trouble, depression, and anxiety."

The other day as I was sitting in a cafe, a man sitting behind me placed a call to his adult daughter. Because he had turned on the speaker phone, I overheard the conversation. She asked him why he had not called earlier and why it had been a few days since she had heard from him. He explained that his cell phone battery had gone dead and he had to find a way to charge it. With sadness in her voice she responded, "You live everyday hoping to die. Don't you love us? Don't you want to be with us? Why do you want to die? We haven't heard from you in days and before that weeks. You have no desire to do anything or to help yourself." He did not reply but just listened. The conversation went on as she pleaded with him to find the strength to live. I gathered from the rest of the dialogue that he had a drinking problem and was homeless. Hearing their conversation brought me such sadness. I wanted to talk to him and find out the reasons for his indifference. Which of his Soul-Nourishing Foods™ was out of balance? Was it money? Career? Joy? Spirituality? It was obvious to me that he had a loving family who were concerned about him. However, somewhere along the way, his Soul-Nourishing Foods became unbalanced as was his life. Unfortunately, it was not my place to meddle. Perhaps all he needed was a hug and someone to allow him to express his pain and frustrations.

Geneen Roth, an author on the topic of eating disorders, said "Feelings never killed anyone. Not feeling the feelings kills people". People who do not deal with their feelings or their Soul-Nourishing Foods either slowly kill themselves through various addictions or through suicide. For many years, I did not deal with my emotions but rather stuffed them down with food and cigarettes. In my college years there was the addition of binge drinking. It was easier to numb the pain than to journey through the pain.

My life had not unfolded as I had planned. I imagined that by 30, I would be blissfully married with a family. As a result of my life not conforming to my childhood expectations, over the years I gained weight. The weight gain was a result of my unhappiness and not knowing how to positively channel my pain. We may think the pain of facing our troubles is overwhelming but not doing so creates a self-imposed emotional prison. In an effort to avoid dealing with the issues or emotions head-on, we may overcompensate in other areas like our career or our quest for money. The overcompensation is often at the expense of other areas and relationships.

Today at the age of 42, I am physically and emotionally healthier, living with a great canine companion, unmarried with no children. My life may be different from my young self's fairy tale fantasy, but it is wonderful one.

My intention for this book and for you is to provide information and ideas to enhance your Soul-Nourishing Foods so that you may find your way faster to a happier, calmer and more balanced life. I hope my life stories can remind you that you are not alone.

CHAPTER 1

Self Care/Inner Joy
Taking Care of the VIP

The number one Soul-Nourishing Food™

You may be wondering why this chapter is so important to finding a blissful life. The main issue that many of us face is the habit of putting the needs of others ahead of our own. You may be a single parent, a caregiver to your parents, a people-pleaser, or just someone who enjoys taking care of others. This may come at the expense of yourself and your happiness. If you have traveled by plane, you know that on every flight, there is an in-flight lecture, instructing you that in the event of an emergency, the oxygen mask will fall from its compartment. You are to put a mask on yourself *before* putting a mask on any other person. The reasoning is that if your oxygen is depleted, you might faint and be of no use to anyone else.

The same analogy applies to each of us. Unfortunately unlike their male counterparts, women are taught from a young age to be caregivers and nurturers. Regardless of gender, it is not selfish to attend to our needs first. Making time for daily exercise, meditation, and nutritious meals provides us with the endurance needed to take on the tasks of the day. Make yourself a priority.

Remember, others learn how to treat us by the way we treat ourselves. When make our physical, emotional, and spiritual needs priorities, this sends a non-verbal signal to others about the level of respect we have for ourselves. Sometimes, we need to resist the lessons from our childhood that robbed us of our self-esteem. When we are happy and content, no word or action can hurt us. We send boomerangs of positivity into the world around us, and in turn, we invite greater positive energy to flood our lives.

What types of practices constitute self-care? Self-care includes exercising, eating right, and finding the time to do things that feed and nourish your soul. Are there hobbies you have wanted to do? Have you fed your family but neglected to feed yourself? Like some of you, I have been guilty of neglecting my needs. I love to take care of those who mean the most to me. Helping others validates me and makes me feel as if I am making a positive impact in someone's life. But should it be at my own expense? There are so many ways to nurture ourselves. We will explore these methods in later chapters.

> *"Where focus goes, energy flows. And if you don't take the time to focus on what matters, then you're living a life of someone else's design." —Tony Robbins, entrepreneur and bestselling author.*

Some people settle in their lives, believing that their fate is predestined. This is a limiting belief. I believe that life can always be improved. We can choose to live a mediocre life or a spectacular one, but living a spectacular life requires a healthy balance of our Soul-Nourishing Foods.

The relationship between self-care and inner joy is intertwined. Joy cannot be predicated on another person or thing. It can only be found within ourselves. In my twenties, I was so unhappy, lonely, and bored that I moved from Hoboken to Boston in search of happiness. I thought by changing my geography, I was going to change my life and thus my happiness. While I did enjoy my time in Boston, after a couple of years, I once again I found myself unhappy, lonely, and bored. Why? Because a change in geography did not correct the problem. It was not knowing how to be content with myself when others were not available to participate in activities with me. There were a myriad of activities available to me, but I did not want to experience them alone. Had I been comfortable enough with myself to participate in them, I would have widened my circle of friends and broadened my experiences.

Reflecting upon my own life, there is advice I wish I had received or had heeded much earlier. To commemorate my nephew's sixteenth birthday, I wrote him a letter with a compilation of these life lessons. One piece of advice I gave him was, "Relationships do not define you." Many people in relationships are very unhappy. They ponder whether having someone else's life, someone else's spouse, or being single would make them happy. Would making a change bring them happiness? Perhaps, but it would be fleeting. After the newness of the change wore off, they would find themselves unhappy once again, as I did when I moved to Boston. Constantly relying on external forces for your bliss will lead you on a lifetime path of unhappiness and discontent.

I was searching for love when I met my ex-boyfriend, Eric. I had been single for a few years and had a yearning for love and companionship. Meeting him made me hopeful. Would he be the missing puzzle piece to my life? Would he be my life companion? I had a preset view of what a relationship should be. When we were apart, I would make a list of all the wonderful things I had always wanted to do with a companion. My focus was in creating a perfect relationship, rather than letting the relationship unfold organically. My expectation was for him to complete me, and in doing so, I would finally be happy. It was unrealistic and unfair to impose such pressure on him. He was a busy, hardworking, single father, working to create a space for love in his life. My life was more flexible than his, and my responsibilities were fewer. At the beginning of my relationship with Eric, a great friend advised me to "stay busy." I did not understand what she meant. Had I lived a life of fullness on my own, I would not have placed such high expectations on a relationship. When we have enough distance from a situation, we can see things with more clarity. Eric is an amazing man I was blessed to have had in my life, even if only for a short time. My unrealistic perceptions of what a relationship should be caused me frequent disappointments. Had I filled the void I felt with Soul-Nourishing Foods, our relationship may have blossomed into something wonderful and long-lasting.

Have you ever lost yourself in a relationship? Before meeting Eric, I was regularly working out and practicing yoga. My nutrition was stellar. As with many couples who begin dating, we indulged frequently in rich foods that were not part of our normal diets. I was no longer eating in a manner that was good for my body and mind. Food can greatly affect mood. As our relationship progressed, his schedule became more erratic, and we began to spend less time together. The less we saw of each other, the more alone I felt. The feeling of loneliness became my excuse to stop exercising, practicing yoga, and I filled the void in my life with unhealthy eating. I spiraled into unhappiness, which led to me to ending the relationship.

Upon reflecting on where things went wrong, I faced the fact that I had relinquished control over my own joy. I had delegated my joy to him. A common mistake we often make is putting our lives on hold or sacrificing ourselves while waiting for a partner to make us whole. The fairy tales we heard growing up taught women that they need saving and that they would experience "happily ever after" once their Prince Charming found them. Conversely, those same fairy tales taught men that their mission in life is to save women from unhappiness. Both men and women may want someone to tell them "you complete me." When I first purchased my condo, I was asked why I did not wait until marriage. I replied, "What if I never get married? Am I to avoid living until then?"

The loss of the relationship was painful. In my heart, I believed I had found the elusive love that was going to "complete" me. That was not the case. But people come into our lives for reasons we may not be privy to at the moment. Who knew he would be the catalyst for my journey of self-completion? He was the mirror I needed to help me see and cultivate the joy that is already in me.

How did I accomplish that, you may ask? It has been attained through a great deal of solitude and self-reflection. I have learned to face and work through my emotions, rather than to avoid them. Most of us can remember hearing our parents tell us, "Stop crying," or "There's nothing to cry about." Others said, "Don't cry; have a cookie," or "Real men don't cry. Toughen up!" These statements have taught us how to avoid painful emotions at all costs. The better choice would be to constructively allow our bodies to release the frustration and sadness. For some, frustration or stress may cause us to shed unwanted tears. It is the body's way of releasing the stress and tension. In the months following the breakup, I cried more than at any other time in my life and sought the help of a therapist. I learned that crying was my body releasing years of suppressed tears. Prior to this experience, I, like so many others, tried to numb my feelings with alcohol, food, or nicotine when crying was a healthier alternative. The most constructive way to deal with difficult feelings is to attend to them and to experience and release the emotion. Tackling the emotion rather than avoiding it is more productive.

Here are a few more tools you can use to enhance joy. When used together and regularly, they are powerful.

Journaling

Journaling is a wonderful tool in dealing with emotions. The act of writing allows you to express feelings, whether good or bad, and without judgment. When you choose to suppress negative feelings, your body finds ways of releasing them through depression, pain, illness, or disease. If you are not comfortable talking with someone close to you, with a therapist, or with a health coach, pull out a journal and release the emotion onto paper and out of your body. Regular journaling is cathartic. The bonus is you will have a memoir of your life. Looking back on some of my earlier journal entries helps me recall a memory or illustrates how far I have grown emotionally.

Gratitude Journal

Another type of journal to consider is a gratitude journal. The journaling described above is about releasing emotions while a gratitude journal is where you record things, big or small, for which you are grateful. When life seems difficult, completing a gratitude journal reminds you of all the things going well in your life which you may have overlooked. Each night write down three things for which you are grateful. You may be grateful for a sunshine filled day that allowed you to be outdoors, or you may be grateful for talking and laughing with a good friend. Gratitude for the small things in life yields a bounty of joy when you can see that your life is full of little miracles. Find contentment in the little things in life. Winning the state lottery may bring immense but temporary joy. Yet, a daily collection of little positive things may help you realize you have already won the jackpot – a jackpot of happiness.

Meditation

A friend recommended meditation to me because my mind is always racing. It may be bombarded with mental to-do lists or negative self-talk. Meditation is a practice of clearing your mind for a few minutes each day. Just as we shut down our computer each night to give it a rest, meditation is a reboot for the brain. There are many successful people who meditate daily some of whom include Oprah Winfrey, Rupert Murdock, Bill Ford, Arianna Huffington, rapper 50 Cent, and Russell Simmons. Russell Simmons recently released a book titled *Success in Stillness: Meditation Made Simple*. What these successful people found was that when they clear their minds through the act off meditating, creative ideas or thoughts flood in. Meditation has health benefits. It lowers blood pressure and heart rate because you are slowing down your body down thus lowering cortisol in your body. A Harvard Medical School study showed that meditation "can switch on and off some genes linked to stress and immune function."[2] By stilling your mind, you also find a deeper or renewed connection with yourself and your intuition.

Listening to Your Intuition

Intuition is a very powerful tool within all of us. It is the little voice inside that lets us know or feel when something is not right or when there is imminent danger. There may be times you have had an intuitive thought about something going on with your body and you sought medical confirmation. Intuition is within us since our inception. However, along the path from childhood to adulthood, we learn to ignore or to doubt it. We need to rediscover and connect with that little inner voice as doing so will help us find our joy. Arianna Huffington, the President and Editor-in-Chief of the Huffington Post and the author of the book Thrive writes:

> *"Even when we're not at a fork in the road, wondering what to do and trying to hear that inner voice, our intuition is always there, always reading the situation, always trying to steer us the right way. But can we hear it? Are we paying attention? Are we living a life that keeps the pathway to our intuition unblocked? Feeding and nurturing our intuition, and living a life in which we can make use of its wisdom, is one key way to thrive, at work and in life."*[3]

Oprah, imparted many great life tips to her viewers. One tip she repeatedly told viewers was "Doubt means don't." She said that intuition sometimes comes to us in a very faint whisper, and when we ignore it, the intuitive message grows louder and louder until one day it figuratively smacks us on the head. By that time, it may be too late. I have heard those intuitive messages a few times in my life. Sometimes I ignored them because I was fearful to believe their message and other times I heeded it. Almost always, my intuition was spot on. Trust in yourself, and pay attention to those little whispers. They just may save your life.

Vision Boards

Visualization is used by many successful people to realize their goals. Many Olympians spend time visualizing winning a gold medal in their sport. Others like Diana Nyad, the long distance swimmer who recently swam 110 miles from Havana, Cuba, to the Florida Keys, use visualization as part of their training program. A vision board is where you paste words or pictures of things that mean something to you or that you are aspiring to or for. It can be created using a computer or poster board. It helps you visualize your goals and dreams. Suppose your dream is to visit Paris someday. On your vision board, you may post a picture of a plane, a Paris scene or the words, "Paris." Perhaps you have a vision of a type of life you aspire to have. You would post words that describe that life or paste pictures that are representative of that life.

In the movie "Under the Tuscan Sun," Diane Lane plays Frances, a woman going through a painful divorce who, during a trip to Tuscany, spontaneously purchases a Tuscan fixer upper. During one of her bouts of loneliness, she laments to her real estate agent, Martini, and lists all the things she wishes she had and what she visualized for the home. He tells her about a section of the Alps that is impossibly steep but a train track was built there to connect Vienna and Venice before there was a train in existence that could make the trip. The tracks were built because the people had faith a train would one day exist to make the trip. Fast forward a few months and Frances and Martini are at a wedding that is held on her property. Martini points out that Francis got everything she previously had told him she wanted.

The vision board is where you build your "tracks" for your dream. Looking at it gets you to subconsciously begin to build the train needed that one day will carry you to your destination. I heard of someone who had posted a picture on his vision board of his dream house. He forgot about the home and had moved a few times since he made the vision board. As he was unpacking his boxes in the new house he and his family had moved into, he came upon his old vision board. What came as a big surprise was that the picture of his dream house was the exact house he and his family had just move into! He never made the connection until he saw the vision board.

> *"We must be willing to let go of the life we planned*
> *so as to have the life that is waiting for us".*
> -*Joseph Campbell, an American mythologist, writer and lecturer*

Mental Shift

Negativity can have a profound impact on one's health and direction of one's joy. For some people the practice of positive thinking comes naturally and for others the opposite is true. How does one's state of mind affect one's health? Consider the person who has been diagnosed with cancer, or has been paralyzed. Someone who has a strong positive attitude may have their cancer enter remission, or if paralyzed, may walk again. Conversely, others who feel defeated may have a very different prognosis. Henry Ford once said, "Whether you think you can or you think you can't – you're right." A good friend was recently diagnosed with stage 4 cancer which carries a 30% survival rate. He told no one of his cancer as he did not want pity or sadness during his time of treatment. A couple of us found out after we realized we had not heard from him in a bit. His request was for no visitors. He maintained a positive mental state even though the chemotherapy ravaged his body. He visualized himself beating the cancer. The other day he called me to report that he is 100% cancer free! He felt having the cancer diagnosis was a blessing in disguise because it lead to his making healthy dietary changes to improve his health and to strengthen his immune system. His attitude was awe inspiring and was a reminder to make lemonade out of life's lemons.

Baths

I had always preferred showers over baths. It was incomprehensible to me that anyone would want to sit in water for 15-20 minutes and do nothing. I have since changed my stance on baths as I have come to understand the stress relief they provide. Most days, we rush through life. We rarely take the time to relax, to "smell the roses," and to decompress. Sometimes slowing down and tuning out external noise is needed. A hot aromatherapy bath can be just what the doctor ordered to relieve stress. Remember those commercials in the '80s in which the woman begs the brand of bubble bath to take her away? Find your preferred bath product to take you away for just a few minutes. It can be a cup or two of Epsom salts, scented bath salts, bath balls, essential oils, bubble baths, or rose petals. Light candles or dim the lights and play soft relaxation/meditation music. Some people like to read a book or sip a glass of wine during their bath. Whatever you do, turn the phones off, shut the door (lock it if you have to) and forget about the world. The next 15-20 minutes are for you and you alone. Sit in the hot bath and forget all your problems and cares. The hot bath can make you drowsy so take care that the water is not excessively deep to prevent drowning in the event you fall asleep.

After soaking in the tub, rinse off and slather some almond oil or body lotion on your body. Your skin will thank you. This is the time to show your body love and appreciation for its beauty, flaws and all. If you are experiencing sleep difficulty, a nightly bathing ritual will help. Avoid turning on the television or the computer as exposure to the bright screen stimulates a nerve pathway from the eye to the part of the brain that controls our hormones and body temperature. A recent study at Ohio State University, found that exposure to unnatural light cycles may contribute to an increased risk for depression.[4]

Date Yourself

Yes, I am sure this sounds very strange to you as it sounded strange to me when it was suggested by my therapist. She asked me to take myself out weekly and to do something that I found interesting and fun. This is an opportunity to do something without the influence of others. You can do whatever you want without someone complaining that they are bored or wanting to move on. You can spend the day at your favorite museum, walk around the city or your town, go hiking, go to the zoo, visit a coffeehouse and write your next novel, go to a music concert or do whatever inspires you because this is your time. If you have a family, ask your spouse, find a relative or baby sitter to watch the kids even for a few hours, or work something out with another single parent and agree to trade babysitting duties. Exploring things that you enjoy will make you feel happier. In the beginning unaccompanied outings made me feel lonely, but after some time, the loneliness dissipated. I began looking forward to these solo excursions.

For my 40th birthday, I had the opportunity to go to Hawaii. A friend was traveling there on business, and we had discussed arriving three days prior so that we had five solid days there. However, my friend's work itinerary changed after I had booked my ticket. I tried very hard to find a friend who would be able to make a very last minute trip with me during a work week. Unfortunately, no one had the flexibility to take time off. I had contemplated not going as traveling alone to Hawaii seemed depressing for a single gal. Thankfully, I found the fortitude to go and had the best time! I met so many people on that trip and keep in touch with them today. Had I gone with my friend as originally planned, I would not have made these new friendships.

Therapy

For many, the topic of therapy may be uncomfortable. There is absolutely no shame in therapy or in seeking the help of a trained psychotherapist. I wish I had seen a therapist earlier in life. Instead of scheduling an appointment with one, I felt ashamed. In our culture there is a stigma associated with mental illness. I believe everyone should see a therapist at some point in their lives. Why? Because therapy helps you deal constructively with your issues. Our parents did not have a manual for how to raise us. They did the very best they could, and despite the best of intentions, there may have been periods that negatively affected us. We are all unique in the way we process words and situations. Words spoken to you may have one effect while those same words spoken to your sibling may have had a different effect. You may have experienced a situation which may have led you to not know how to deal with stress or anxiety. If you were bullied or experienced some form of abuse, a trained therapist can assist you with healing the emotional pain that arises from these traumatic events.

Beginning with inception of the Mental Health Parity and Addiction Equality Act of 2008 and now with the parity law's enforcement under the Affordable Care Act (ACA), mental health and substance abuse benefits must be covered comparably to how medical and surgical benefits are covered. This means if an insurance carrier covers a certain number of doctor visits or a specific length of in-patient treatments for medical and surgical care, the number of visits or length of time must be the same for mental health and substance abuse coverage. Mental health and drug treatment is also one of the required ten categories of Essential Health Benefits (EHB) that all insurers must offer in the individual, small group market and in states expanding their Medicaid programs.[5] Additionally, pre-existing conditions are now covered. I began therapy immediately after I met Eric. I wanted to be my best version for me and for him so we could lead happy lives together. In order to do that I had to deal with lingering trust issues. My therapist, Robin, helped me see a different side to an argument or issue I was facing and gave me the tools to work with to right the situation or modify the behavior. Even after the relationship with Eric ended, Robin helped me deal with my grief and loss. She was also instrumental in arming me with great tools to strengthen my inner joy.

Perhaps you are lonely. You may not want to share feelings and emotions with those you love due to a feeling of shame, of fear, or of not wanting to be perceived as a burden. Unloading your problems on friends often can be taxing on even your best friendships. Your friends may not be equipped to help you. They may be dealing with their own problems, and taking on yours can be overwhelming and cause them to disappear from your life. The extraordinary friends will not leave, but most others will. That is why a trained therapist is so vital. Therapists are paid to hear your problems and to provide you with a safe place to cry and de-stress. They will provide an impartial perspective, and you may realize what you thought was insurmountable is actually manageable. We all need a release valve. Repressed feelings can cause you to explode at random at someone you love. These types of feelings may cause you to do something dangerous to yourself or to others.

If you have insurance, find a therapist who accepts your coverage. The visit to the therapist may cost you a small copay or a reduced office visit fee, depending on your plan's benefits. If you do not have insurance, there are therapists who will charge you on a sliding scale that is based on your income. Look online for training clinics, typically located in universities, where graduate students prepare to become clinical or counseling psychologists. They are supervised by licensed psychologists. When choosing a therapist, find one who will work with your financial situation and who specializes in the area you need help with such as eating disorders, relationships, abuse, general psychology, helping you with creativity, anxiety/depression, and LBGT. Find a community mental health center in your area. You can find a support group for a specific issue. There are many options, so please do not feel alone.

Depression does not discriminate. I met a man who is so beautiful on the inside and handsome and strong on the outside. He is handsome in looks and extremely intelligent, yet he is crippled with depression. The reason for his depression is because he did not feel he was where he "should" be in comparison to his friends and other medical school classmates. He is a medical doctor, yet he cannot see how comparison to others is very dangerous and how food affects the body, brain and hence, mood. Not surprisingly, his diet is poor. I say not surprisingly because most physicians receive very little training in nutrition and many do not believe that food is medicine. This particular doctor's diet is heavy in refined sugar, caffeine, high fructose corn syrup, wheat (most likely the GMO variety), and milk, which I would bet is laden with hormones. It is not surprising to me that he would be suffering multiple bouts of depression that mentally cripples him. I know this to be true because it happened to me.

I spent nearly my whole life mildly depressed. Many times I wanted to avoid socialization and connecting with others. I preferred to drown my sorrows in tubs of chemical, hormone, and high fructose corn syrup laden ice cream and other salty, highly processed snacks. During these dark periods, I prayed for a solution to my depression. For a long time I did not realize that my circumstance could be changed by some easy tweaks to my diet.

Years ago on The Oprah Show, a doctor, named Dr. Oz began to appear regularly. It was with one episode that I began to claw my way out of the well of desperation and depression. Dr. Oz discussed what high fructose corn syrup was and how it caused depression. Upon hearing this surprising bit of information, I jumped up from the couch and immediately went to the kitchen to read the food labels of all the products I had there. To my shock, every item I had contained high fructose corn syrup as well as many other unrecognizable and unpronounceable ingredients.

After a little more research about food and mood, I soon discovered that dairy was another culprit. Without hesitation, I made the decision to help myself by discarding these poisonous foods. The pain of the depression far outweighed the pleasure that I was deriving from these fake foods. With each passing day, I began to feel the cloud of darkness lift, and little by little I felt a bit lighter and happier. I began to reach out to those from whom I had retreated. Even though I was feeling better, I still experienced cravings, but this time I made sure my snack foods did not contain high fructose corn syrup. While my depression greatly improved, it did not totally disappear. It would be a few more years before I received my official diagnosis of celiac disease, an autoimmune disease caused by the proteins in wheat, barley, and rye. I was experiencing a lightness in spirit that I had never known before.

There are many of you who do not believe food is medicine. I understand. Until that life changing television segment, I thought the notion that diet soda could make you fat or foods can cause depression was preposterous. Having experienced it first hand, I am now a huge believer in the power of food and how it can be used to heal our bodies.

Perfectionism

Let's circle back to my depressed doctor friend. He was depressed because he felt he did not match up to his friends' accomplishments. In comparison to his friends, his life seemed inadequate. Perfection is something that he seems to strive for in so many areas of his life. He works daily on maintaining his perfectly chiseled physique. He is a licensed medical doctor from another country who has come to the US to become US board certified. He, like many foreign doctors I have come to know, believes that the US medical system is the gold standard of medicine. He has had many successes but his successes do not live up to his high standards. This makes him depressed and he feels like a failure.

Striving for perfection is dangerous because perfection is elusive in nature. I lived my life wanting perfection; all it did was make me more depressed when perfection was not achieved. When you set very high expectations for yourself, for your relationships and for your life, disappointments are more frequent and happiness is fleeting. Why? Because you will never be satisfied with the status quo and will constantly want to attain the unattainable instead of enjoying the moment – the present. The time I spent trying to achieve perfection brought me stress and unhappiness. In working with a therapist, I learned that my house did not have to be showroom ready each time I had planned for a visitor. My hair did not have to be always perfectly cut or styled, and I did not need to plan out my life in detail in order to ensure it was a great one. When your attention is always looking to the future, you miss the experiences that are happening in the present. Focusing on the present and giving up on perfectionism has made me more relaxed, less anxious and much happier. Being more flexible instead of trying to control all aspects of life removes a great deal of self-imposed pressure. Doing so does not mean that I accept mediocrity. Instead it means that I let go of less important things, accept new and unexpected paths, and enjoy my life more fully. You never know where a new path may lead. It may just be to a joy you never thought possible.

The secret of happiness is to count your blessings while others are adding up their troubles. – William Penn

CHAPTER 2

Socialization

Why Can't I Just Be Alone?

We are all social beings with a primal need to feel a sense of belonging. For a good portion of my life, I never felt I belonged in any one group. Feeling out of place was partly due to the fact that I could not relate to many multigenerational Americans. I am a first generation American raised by two immigrants with different values, interests and beliefs. My father is from South America and my mother is Eastern European. My friends and their families enjoyed football and baseball while my family preferred soccer and fencing. My friends watched mainstream television shows and movies while we watched Nova, Discovery Channel, and the occasional movie. What I did not realize was that we all need to find our tribe. A tribe is a community in which the members share like-minded thoughts and interests. Your tribe can be your family, a group of friends, the parishioners of your church – anywhere you feel a connection.

Connection and interaction are integral pieces to your quality of life and to your health. Friendships can bolster your immune system by reducing stress related illnesses. When we are frustrated or angry, most often we feel better after talking out the situation with a friend. According to the American Institute of Stress, "Laboratory studies show that when subjects are subjected to stress, emotional support reduces the usual sharp rise in blood pressure and increased secretion of damaging stress related hormones."[6]

Friendships also have an impact on our longevity. Dan Buettner author of *The Blue Zones -- Lessons for Living Longer from the People Who've Lived the Longest,* went around the world searching for areas that had the highest concentration of centenarians, those 100 years old and older. He would ask the centenarians what the secret was to their longevity, and they would tell him that socialization was very important to them. When he spoke with Robert Kane, Director of the Center on Aging and the Minnesota Geriatric Education Center at the University of Minnesota in Minneapolis, Robert said:

> *There are some things I'd certainly recommend for what people would call successful aging. One of them is, in fact, to have a sense of social connectedness. Most people enjoy the company of other people, particularly other people who they feel care about them. That seems to give you a sense of well-being, whether that raises your endorphin level or lowers your cortisol level.*

During Dan's visit with the people of Okinawa, he met a group of women who had a moai, loosely translated as "meeting for a common purpose" who met regularly to talk, laugh and to support each other. One woman he spoke with said, "It's much easier to go through life knowing there is a safety net." Dan writes that, "On average, an American has only two close friends he or she can count on, recently down from three, which may contribute to an increasing sense of stress." By contrast, these Okinawan women live almost 8 percent longer than their American counterparts. Why? Because every afternoon, when they get together, they shed all the chronic stress in their lives with each other. Laughter is so important for cardiovascular health because it reduces stress[7].

A few months ago, I returned from an incredible weekend of sister- and brother-hood among my "family" at our alma mater, New York Military Academy (NYMA). It had been about twenty-five years since I had seen most of my former classmates. When we arrived at alumni weekend and reunited, it was as if no time had passed as we instantly fell back into sync with one another. Looking around the room, all I saw were happy faces bonding and reminiscing with their fellow former classmates. It did not matter whether or not we had been in the same circles because we shared a common experience, boarding at a military academy. During the weekend, I spent twenty-seven hours laughing, connecting, and catching up with old friends, all of whom I consider family. It is those types of relationships that feed our souls and bring us health.

How does a strong social circle and connection to others affect health?

New York Military Academy was a moai for my classmates and me. Cadets entered anywhere from fifth to twelfth grade. Imagine living with your friends day in and day out? You do most things together, and you spend time building shared memories. I spent five years with these people, and we had seen each other at our highs and at our lows and had shared a common experience that no one outside of our group could relate to or understand. The friendships made in our youth are important to our health. It is through these lifelong bonds that we have a sense of belonging -- of camaraderie -- that makes our stress levels go down, but it is also without these people that we feel sad.

For many of you, your loneliness may be attributed to the fact that you never felt you fit in during your high school years or perhaps you have outgrown the friendships you had with your childhood friends. For others, you may be new to the country, neighborhood or workplace. I think we all have a deep rooted desire to fit in, to feel validated, and to be seen.

I have been coming to a local coffeehouse in town for the past few weeks to write and have noticed that many people come here to work. They could easily stay home, go to the library, or work in a quieter environment. So why are they all here? I think it is to be surrounded by other humans and to have the ability to interact with each other on occasion. I have met some interesting people those times when I was sharing a table with four other people who all had their laptops and books out to work. I have met people with varying interests - those studying to become doctors here in the US, others with an interest in running farms in other countries. As I come to frequent this location, I begin to see familiar faces. Even though I do not know these people, being around them gives me a sense of community.

In his book, *The Blue Zones Project*, Dan Buettner writes about how many centenarians have robust social circles. Having good, solid, dependable friends is crucial. Surrounding yourself with positive and fun people is also key. Have you ever noticed how stressed you feel when that one negative friend calls? I had that "friend." Every time she called, my stomach was in knots because I knew that I would hear another story of drama, and gloom and doom that would make me feel either sad or frustrated. No matter how much I tried to help her, she continued to go down the same road and repeat the same mistakes. She was not happy unless she had chaos and drama while I yearned for peace, calm, and a drama-free life.

The key to good friendships is to find compatible individuals who are traveling along the same path or are already where you want to be. Remember, "Like attracts like." That is the Law of Attraction.

Technology & Isolation

With technology, isolation is becoming more and more prevalent. People are spending more time texting and communicating via electronic devices than meeting with their friends in person. Additionally, if you go to any bar or restaurant, you will see more people engaging on their phones than with their dining companions. Yet every day, I hear how lonely and disconnected people are feeling. Just like you, others want to feel heard and to feel special. There is nothing worse than telling a story to your friend while he/she is texting with someone else, or seems more interested in the social media feed than in you. Work on shutting off your phone during time spent with others. Focus your attention on the other person. When you are present in the moment, you develop stronger connections and a greater sense of happiness.

Pets – the Story of Sasha

Eight years ago, Sasha, my darling Yorkie, came into my life quite unexpectedly. I had been wearing a heart rate monitor in an effort to improve my fitness. One evening, I was sitting on my couch when I began to feel palpitations. When I glanced down, the monitor showed a reading of 215 heartbeats/minute. To give some perspective, a normal resting heart rate in adults ranges from 60 to 100 beats a minute.[8] Since I was clearly not working out, seeing such a high rate frightened me. I decided I would get dressed and walk over to the emergency room that was a few blocks away.

Unfortunately, I had to call 911 instead. The ambulance arrived and the paramedics took me to the hospital where I received a battery of tests. After several hours with no diagnosis, the ER doctor advised that I go home and make an appointment with a cardiologist to do further investigation into my situation. Finding a cardiologist who had immediate availability proved difficult. Finally after many phone calls, I located one cardiologist who was able to see me the very next day.

My mother drove me to the doctor's office. Another series of tests namely EKGs, treadmill stress test, and heart rate monitors were administered yet still no abnormalities were found. Finally, the seasoned doctor called me into his office and asked my mother to wait outside. He said to me, "I believe you are stressed" to which I replied, "What do I have to be stressed about? I am self-employed, make my own hours, am single, I travel often and enjoy my life." Looking at me over his reading glasses he said, "Miss Gavino, we have not been able to find anything wrong with your heart. I am recommending that you get a dog." In amazement I responded, "If I wasn't stressed before, I am going to be stressed now! Having a dog would disrupt my single life not to mention diminish my travel. There is no way I am getting a dog!"

After I marched out of the doctor's office in frustration, my mother wanted to hear what the doctor had advised. I related the conversation and of course, she relayed the information to my father. For the next two days, I was hounded (no pun intended!) by my folks to get a dog. In an effort to placate them, I finally I agreed to look at a few dogs. Mom and I visited a breeder who had a couple of eight week old Yorkies – one male, one female. They were so tiny that the thought of having to care for such a little living creature frightened me. But before I knew what was happening, the little female Yorkie was packed up to come home with me.

To tell you I cried is an understatement. I cried from the fear of having to care for this little life. I did not want my mom to leave because I did not have the experience to care for a puppy. After giving me the cliff notes version on pet care, she left me with Sasha the next day knowing I would be able to handle my new responsibility.

Sasha is now eight years old and the love of my life! During my bouts of depression, she would do something to make me laugh. She has taught me lessons on patience, sharing, and compassion. Because of her, I was forced to take daily walks and to learn how to care for something outside myself. Today we take four mile walks together. I owe my life to this little ten pound, spunky, willful, loving dog. When life is tough or stressful, holding and petting her melts the stress away. I never realized how lonely I was until she came into my life. She is a blessing to me, and I am so grateful to the cardiologist who gave me the most brilliant prescription.

Pets have an amazing ability to absorb our energy. Whenever I have been stressed for a period of time, I have noticed that Sasha begins to have digestive issues that seem to resolve themselves around the time that I am no longer feeling the stress or anxiety.

I have a friend who whose dog was diagnosed with cancer in the same week that she, herself, was diagnosed with the same disease.

They both underwent chemotherapy together. After treatment, the cancer in both owner and dog went into remission.

There have been numerous stories of pets developing the same type of cancers or other diseases in the same locations as their owners.

I believe that our pets are so in tune with energy that they cannot help but take on our negative energy. Have you ever noticed that when a dog senses a dangerous person, it becomes aggressive? How does your pet react to an impending storm? How is dog trainer, Caesar Milan, able to calm even the most ferocious of dogs with only his energy while other excitable people spur excitement in their pets without even making a sound?

When Sasha was very sick a few years ago, her holistic vet instructed me to get calming herbs. I asked him how much I should give her to which he responded, "It is not for her but for you." I was taken aback by his comment, but he could sense my stress and anxiety over her worsening condition and needed me to manage my stress so she could recover. Once I began to understand the reasoning behind his comment and changed the energy I was projecting, she was able to recover quickly.

There is a growing trend in the number of one-person households. In 2005, twenty-six percent of households in the US were one-person households. With more and more people living alone, loneliness may increase. Having a pet can reduce the feeling of loneliness.[9] The reason pets can be an invaluable source of healing is because they provide unconditional love which can be helpful to people with depressive tendencies.[10] Pets provide us with a sense of responsibility as they need regular feeding, routine activity, and an abundance of love.

An experiment by Kerstin Uvnas-Moberg, an M.D. and Ph.D. at Uppsala University in Sweden, found "that women and their dogs experienced similar increases in oxytocin levels after ten minutes of friendly contact."[11]

With so many health benefits to pet ownership, perhaps you may want to expand your family by adopting a pet. When adopting, please be sure to find a reputable organization. There are a number of shelters and rescue organizations full of loving and caring pets in need of good homes. I caution against purchasing dogs from pet stores as many of those animals are products of puppy mills, where they are bred in sub-par and cruel conditions.[12] I encourage you to welcome a pet into your home as a pet will surely repay your love in so many ways.

Friendships in all forms – human or non-human – have a profound effect on our health. Go forth and find your moai, your tribe, your Sasha.

CHAPTER 3

Relationships
Looking for Connection

Humans have an innate need to be loved. When we are frustrated with our relationships, the emotions we are feeling may create stress and cause us to seek food and other vices for solace and avoidance. The emotions we are feeling may create stress in our bodies. Conversely, when we are content in relationships, we feel happy, and a hormone called oxytocin is released in our brains giving us a euphoric feeling.

We all crave relationships with another person. It is natural to want to be loved and to love. However, in order to receive the love we so desire, we must nourish the most important relationship we will ever have - the relationship with ourselves. As mentioned in Chapter 1, many of us are givers who put the needs of others ahead of our own. This act of self-sacrifice is akin to not putting the airplane oxygen mask on ourselves before putting it on our loved ones. When we do not care for ourselves, we cannot properly take care of anyone else.

On my journey to self-improvement, I contacted a couple of my ex-boyfriends and asked them for the gift of clarity on what I could change to be able to find love. I met each of them in high school, and we have remained great friends after our breakups. In speaking with them, each told me the same thing. My biggest flaw was putting their needs ahead of my own. Knowing how giving I was, they knew they could take advantage of my generous nature. They would have preferred it if I put my needs before theirs and that I had a little more self-confidence.

That was an eye-opening experience. I had always thought I projected self-confidence since I was a sole proprietor working in a male-dominated industry, having achieved success and "the American Dream." But I thought more about their comments and realized that perhaps there was a kernel of truth in what they were telling me. One said that when he was an EMT, he and his fellow paramedics were trained that in a crisis, there were procedures of scene safety they must follow. Their own safety was considered most important, followed by their partner's, the first responders', and only after all of them were safe, the patient's. It is the EMT's job to rest, eat well, and assess the situation to avoid harm to themselves. Without the EMT putting himself/herself first, the patient would not stand a chance of survival.

Reflecting on my friend's EMT training to put himself first, I realized that by contrast I had put myself last not only in my relationships but in my career as well. There were times when I would skip meals if I had a great deal of client work. Skipping meals produced headaches or fatigue because I failed to care for myself first. Not setting clear time boundaries had me working into the evenings, weekends, and even holidays depriving me of much needed mental and physical rest. My need to please people and to feel validation motivated me to do those things voluntarily.

I will always be thankful to my two dear friends who gave me that gift of clarity as it made all the difference in the world and caused a mental shift. Now when situations or relationships present themselves, I no longer seek validation through putting the needs of others ahead of my own.

Motivational speaker, Tony Robbins, cites this need for significance and validation among the needs he feels all humans share. We will aim to fulfill some or all these needs at different times in our lives. As excerpted from Tony's website, he writes that these Six Human Needs are:

1. *Certainty*: *assurance you can avoid pain and gain pleasure*
2. *Uncertainty/Variety*: *the need for the unknown, change, new stimuli*

3. **Significance**: *feeling unique, important, special or needed*
4. **Connection/Love**: *a strong feeling of closeness or union with someone or something*
5. **Growth**: *an expansion of capacity, capability or understanding*
6. **Contribution**: *a sense of service and focus on helping, giving to and supporting others[13]"*

Based on the Tony's Six Human Needs and what my former boyfriends imparted about me, my dominant human needs are significance and connection/love. Once I had this realization, I was better able to find a balance between getting those dominant human needs met and putting myself first through self-care. In Section II of this book, I will give you the tools you need to practice more self-care so you can put yourself first and be better able to give to others of yourself.

Connection

We search out relationships to satisfy our need for connection. The ability to have mature conversations in the areas of sex and intimacy is important in connecting. Relationships can only work if we are able to convey needs and feelings to our partner. When your partner does not respond in a manner that you desire, you may seek to compensate for your feelings of hurt and rejection. Some people turn to food and alcohol, some bury themselves in work, and still others may seek companionship outside the marriage. In one of my relationships, my ex-boyfriend had difficulty expressing emotions. His lack of emotional expression made me feel lonely and insecure. It was in that relationship that I began to understand how people become involved in affairs. I think that if people spoke with their partners about how they are feeling instead of looking outside the relationship for what is lacking, we would experience a decrease in divorces. Relationships are complicated and while this is a simplistic view, I urge you to start a dialogue with your partner if you are feeling a disconnection.

It is equally important to find people who have similar paths and interests. We sometimes fall in love with the idea of love but are too blind to notice that the other person may not be a fit for us. When I met my ex, I thought I had found my soulmate. I wanted this relationship so much that I had ignored some important traits that would make us incompatible. He was regimented while I was not. He needed to schedule our dates in advance while I was more spontaneous. He was emotionally closed while I was emotionally open. These were not minor issues in our relationships. These were issues that were making us both unhappy, but we both wanted so much to make it work that we tried longer than we should have. For me, his rigidness and emotional unavailability were deal breakers. There were times I wanted to see him, but he would turn me down because a visit was not scheduled in advance. The rejection caused me to feel sad and unloved. Yet for him, declining my invitation was not an issue of how he felt about me but rather how schedules made him feel as if he had some order in his life.

Touch is a basic human need and an integral part of relationships. A hand on yours, a hug, or cuddling makes us feel as if we have a connection to another human being. We are a society deprived of touch. In many countries outside the U.S., people kiss each other's cheeks or hug when they meet even if for the first time. Yet I have found that in the U.S., we have the need for personal space and are uncomfortable when others enter that space. Usually we extend our hand to shake the other person's hand or we wave "hello" to them. Touching is reserved for intimate relationships. It is interesting to see that there is a growing field of professional cuddlers who make their living cuddling (absolutely no sex, strictly platonic) others. It may sound strange, but there are many people who are touch-driven and are lacking in that area. Touch was one of the things that attracted me to my ex. As we both are tactile, we found enjoyment in holding and caressing each other's hand. Touch was a way for us to feel a connection.

While touch feels good, there are also health benefits. Studies have shown that a ten second hug may help ease depression, lessen fatigue, boost your immune system, and may even fight infections.[14] If we double the time for hugs from ten seconds to twenty seconds and add ten minutes of handholding, another study shows a significant decrease in stress thereby reducing cortisol levels, blood pressure and heart rates.[15]

Sexual activity is another area where we are starving for connection. In this era of texting, multitasking, television, and video games, we lead very busy lives. Shuttling kids to and from a number of after school activities, working one or two jobs, or caring for aging parents pushes sex down the list of priorities. Connections with those we love may have morphed from romantic love to roommate situations.

Romantic relationship is another area where prioritizing yourself and your partner before your children, your parents, and work is akin to the EMT's putting his/her needs first. It is the complaint I hear from most of my friends. For some couples, the arrival of children brings new responsibilities which dampen their romance. Romantic vacations are less frequent or non-existent as family vacations have replaced them. Work zaps their energy. At home more chores await them – cooking, cleaning up, and preparing for the next day. Consider how much happier you and your partner would be if you instituted a weekly date night and hired a babysitter in order to connect emotionally and sexually again? Time and time again, I have heard complaints of someone not hearing compliments or flattery from their partner and feeling invisible and unimportant. It is at those times that another person may come along and offer words of flattery and compliment that can be a danger to the relationship. We need to take care of our partners and ourselves and really set aside time to connect with each other.

In his book, *The Five Love Languages®*, Dr. Gary Chapman writes that there are five love languages – "quality time, words of affirmation, gifts, acts of service and physical touch." It is through these love languages that we feel loved. Each of us has a preferred love language. Let's assume your partner is expressing his love through his primary love language of acts of service. However, if your love language is physical touch, no act of service will make you feel loved in the manner you need. For example, a husband may express his love by picking up the dry cleaning or taking his wife's car in for routine maintenance or gas. He may wonder why these acts of love are not being embraced. His wife by contrast would feel loved if her husband embraced her or held her hand while they walked. The issue is that they are speaking in two different love languages. Our love language may be like a foreign language that our partner does not understand. Knowing how your partner expresses and receives love is vital to a happy and satisfying relationship.

For those who are single, relationships can be something hoped and longed for. Without a relationship, we can feel as if there is something lacking within ourselves and without a partner, we are somehow not valuable or whole. For most of my adult life, every holiday I would hear "Oh, sweetheart, I just don't know why you're still single. It must be so hard for you," or "One day it will happen for you," or "Why didn't you wait to find a husband before you bought your condo?" It is these comments that while benign in their intention, suggest that somehow my life remain in a holding pattern until I have found a husband, or the holidays must be so difficult to get through being the only single person at the party. And the truth is, that before those comments, I did not feel inadequate for being a "singleton" as coined in the popular novel, *Bridget Jones's Diary*.

In today's world, fifty percent of marriages or more end in divorce, and more and more people are delaying marriage until much later in life. Additionally, in the past, the need for marriage was for procreation of the species and care of offspring, but today there are a growing number of couples electing not to have children. It is important through your practice of self-care to realize that you are enough with or without a relationship. A partner is not there to make you whole – only you can do that for yourself. A partner is there to enhance your life if you choose to have a partner.

It is time that our society come to the realization that people are valuable whether single or coupled, married or divorced, despite their sexual orientation, with or without children. There is not one right or wrong way of being. It is important that you have the relationship that is right for you.

Vulnerability

Being vulnerable with another human being is something that is very difficult for most people - even those in relationships. Vulnerability is transparency. It is letting someone see your soul. It requires you to let go of your fears and to stand in your truth with another person. How many times has your lover asked you to let him or her see your body but you have always denied them their request? How many times have you had the lights turned off during lovemaking or you scurried to cover your body because you were afraid that he or she would no longer be attracted to you if they saw your body during the light of day?

Body image can affect many people and for some it can be debilitating and detrimental not just for yourself but for a relationship. It keeps you from fully experiencing a healthy sexual relationship with your partner. It was something that affected me. I was always looking for the next diet or exercise plan worried that my body would keep me from attracting my mate.

Recently, I had the pleasure of spending the night with a handsome man who has such a beautiful and kind soul. His smile was illuminating and he was kind, gentle and strong. He and I shared a very beautiful and vulnerable night together. After we had been intimate, he asked me to stand up and let him look at my naked form. His request sent a wave of fear through me and caused me to tear up because it terrified me for him to see my body that I felt needed a lot of work. He detected my fear and talked with me about what I was feeling. I explained to him that it was one thing for him to see me naked lying down but another to stand up and be totally exposed without the comfort of a blanket or pillow around me. He reminded me that he had noticed me in Starbucks a couple of days in a row and admired my curvy body. After a few minutes of talking through the fear, I decided to throw caution to the wind. I stood up and let him look at me.

What I saw in his eyes and his body was his lust and desire. He expressed to me verbally how incredible he thought my body was. Then he took me by the hand and led me to the bathroom mirror to show me. I would not glance at our reflection but he moved my head to face the mirror and told me to look. He showed me how beautiful my body was to him. That was the night he changed my entire self-perception. Through his actions, he reminded me that not everyone wants what our society has brainwashed us to believe to be the "perfect" or ideal body. The way he looked at me gave me such confidence and power that I now appreciate and love my body just as it is.

Many of us are afraid of being judged and really seen for who we are - flaws and all. If you have someone in your life you trust, love and feel safe with to be vulnerable, I urge you to let him/her admire you and your figure as it is now. Do not be afraid to stand in your truth. See that your partner loves you just as you are and that he or she doesn't need you to be fitter, more muscular, or thinner in order for him/her to desire and want you. Body image plagues both men and women. When you see your lover look back at you with desire and lust or love, it sets the tone for a very different and equally enjoyable experience. You are no longer worried about your appearance but rather are able to focus on the pleasure of the moment. It will bring you closer to your partner and will make you feel more confident. Confidence translates to being even more attractive to your partner and to others.

If your body is not an issue for you, then perhaps vulnerability means being emotionally vulnerable with that special person. For men, it may be emotional vulnerability that produces a fear in them. Men are raised to be stoic and strong, never to show fear, or to express anything that would be considered weakness. They may fear needing their partner, losing their respect if they share their fears, or worried not being seen as a man. When we are holding back our true selves, we keep from truly connecting with another person. Yes, vulnerability can be scary, but our inability to be vulnerable can also hold us back from creating the intimacy and closeness we desire to have with another person.

Breaking Old Ties and Taking Back Old Promises

When I was 16 years old, I fell in love with a boy who made me feel alive, happy, and loved. I pledged to love him forever. I thought we were destined to be together and no amount of time or distance would sever that love. I had given him my heart. Our relationship ended when he left for college, but with every year that passed after our break-up, subconsciously my heart was still his. We kept in touch over the years and talked about us and our past. Fast forward twenty-seven years and I realized the promise to love him forever, made unconsciously or consciously, was blocking me from the relationship I was meant to have. Why was it that I was consistently going after men who were emotionally unavailable? Was it a subconscious desire for each relationship to fail so as to not break my unspoken promise to my first love? Knowing he was there in the background gave me a sense of security. It was comforting to know there was someone in the world who loved me and still thought I was beautiful. I knew I could get the validation I desired from him. However, as time passed, I knew in my heart it was no longer enough. I wanted something more meaningful, more lasting and permanent that I was never to get from him. When we saw each other at our high school reunion, I was happy to see him as he is and not the idyllic image I had projected in my mind. It was time for me to remove him from the pedestal where I had placed him. Once I saw him with all his flaws, I realized it was time for me to reclaim my heart and undo the promise I had made to him all those years ago.

When you say goodbye to your past loves, you make room for new ones to come in. Let go of all those promises you made whether consciously or subconsciously. If those promises no longer serve you in a positive way, it is a sign that the time has come to let go and move on. It may take you twenty-seven years, as it did for me, but understand that you are on the exact journey you were meant to travel. I have no regrets about loving him, but it was time for me to move forward. Because I am emotionally available, I will be better able to attract a man who is also emotionally available.

"The heart's memory eliminates the bad and magnifies the good" -
Gabriel García Márquez, Love in the Time of Cholera

Non-Romantic Relationships

Relationships do not always have to be of a romantic or sexual nature. They can be relationships you have with your family or your friends. It is said that "hindsight is 20/20" and how very true it is. When I reflect on my life thus far, I see so many things that given the knowledge I have now, I would change. When I was younger, I had a strong need for significance and for validation. Those needs caused me alienate many people whom I used to call friends. I did not know how to be one of the group because I had always been trained to be a leader. I guess that would explain why I am self-employed and never got along well with bosses. I did not make it easy for those friends to want to be part of my life. At the time, my fear of being vulnerable coupled with the emotional pain I was enduring at the time were unmanaged due to the lack of coping tools. Some of my issues stemmed from insecurity while the majority were attributed to the foods which were changing my brain chemistry. Gluten is a very powerful substance. For me and others who have celiac disease, an autoimmune disorder, gluten was greatly affecting my moods. Relief came after many, many years of incorrect diagnoses from the traditional medical community. However by the time I received my diagnosis, it was too late to mend the string of broken friendships. During that low period in my life, my true friends were revealed to me. The friends who remained with me have a significant place in my inner circle today. They have my unending gratitude for their unwavering friendships.

Friendships are vital for us in so many ways. Friends are there to lend an ear when you are down and need to vent, they are there to cheer you up, and they are there to celebrate the happy times with you. My great and longtime friend Patty is one of those beautiful souls whom I have been blessed with in my life. I have known Patty since we were teens. We knew each other's dreams and secret crushes. We have been there for each other through all the break-ups and the milestones. Patty helped me through one of the most difficult times in my life and I can never thank her enough, but with her and many of my other friends who also were by my side, they made my grief a little easier to endure. I continue to try to make amends with some of my other friends whom I alienated in the past. There are a few who have forgiven me. I have made peace with the loss of other friendships. Since then, I have moved forward to make new connections and friendships with others who share the same values.

Like those who severed their relationships with me, you must sever toxic ties. There comes a time in some relationships when you must decide if you should walk away from one that is not serving you emotionally. For some, the idea of quitting anything is difficult especially when you are the one still in love with the other person. But the truth remains that if you are not getting your needs met, are being disrespected, or are being abused in any way, you must walk away and quit the toxic relationship. It is hard, I know, but you will be better for it when you open the space in your heart, clear the toxic and bad energy, and make room for the Universe to bring the right relationship to you.

Letting go of something that meant a lot to you may be difficult at first. You will go through the various stages of grief because, let's face it, it is the death of something. It could be the death of the dream you had of "happily ever after." You may have envisioned a life you wanted with this person and may have even seen a glimpse of what could have been but in reality it was not to be. This is a crucial time for you to practice intensive self-care. It is in the time of break-ups or goodbyes that we can spiral downward in a subconscious attempt to punish ourselves for the failure or demise of a relationship. This is especially true of perfectionists who need everything to be perfect and who may have fears of failure. There is no set timeframe on how long it will take you to get to the other side of your grief. Some experts say not to grieve longer than six weeks. My opinion is to take however long you need as long as it does not exceed six months. Once you exceed six months, you may be carrying a torch for the other person who was not good for you to begin with. See a therapist or talk to someone to help you through this period. Spend time with your friends, keep busy, go back to school, get regular beauty treatments, get back online and date, but whatever you do, avoid feeling sorry for yourself and hurting yourself through food, alcohol, drugs, or nicotine. No one is worth causing yourself harm.

> *"The less you open your heart to others, the more*
> *your heart suffers." – Deepak Chopra*

Appreciation

Wealth means something different to each person. For me the wealthiest people are those who are surrounded by loving and supportive people. The best way to stay wealthy is to consistently show appreciation for those in your life. It takes just a couple of seconds to send a text message telling the other person how you feel. It may be as simple as "I am thinking of you," or "I admire what a great _____ (friend, husband, wife, sister, brother, father, mother) you are." If you want to strengthen your relationships, make appreciation a regular practice and not something you do only on a national holiday. Criticism is more frequently given than appreciation or admiration. When you focus on the positives of others, you attract more positivity into your own life.

One of the keys to a balanced and happy life is the manner in which we care for and nurture the various relationships in our lives. Whether it is the relationship we have with ourselves, or the various types of connections we have with others, these relationships are important to maintain. Allow yourself to be vulnerable, show appreciation, and watch how more enriched your life will become.

CHAPTER 4

Spirituality

What does it Mean to You?

Merriam Webster Dictionary defines spirituality as "sensitivity or attachment to religious values." What does spirituality mean in the context of this book? When I talk about spirituality, I am not referring to any specific religion or lack of religion. I am referring to the thought that there is something out there greater than ourselves. For me, spirituality is the reverence given to everything you do, your connection to others and to everything around you, and for the manner in which you treat those who surround you. It is the way you live your life when you think no one is watching. There is "God" in everything around us. I put God in quotes because I know that there are many reading this book who do not believe in God yet are still spiritual. It does not matter if you believe in the moon, the stars, God, Shiva, Moses, Mother Earth. What matters is that you have an anchor to which you can cling during your darkest hours.

Raised in a Catholic-Judaic household, my parents taught me and my sister about various religions. My father always told us that he did not care what religion we chose to follow when we became adults as long as we believe in something - anything -that will get us through those difficult periods. For him, faith is something to help us when we are at the crossroads of life where one path leads us to despair and darkness while the other leads us to hope and light.

There are many ways to practice spirituality. For some it may be through a religious service of a particular religion, for others it may be through the power of meditation and a gratitude practice. Just because you were raised in a particular religion does not mean you must continue practicing in that faith. Find a spiritual practice that resonates with you and is in line with your beliefs.

Forgiveness

> "Forgiveness is the bedrock of any spiritual practice." — Gabrielle Bernstein, Oprah's Super Soul Sunday

Many of us go through life carrying grudges against those who have wronged us. The problem with holding grudges is that the person you are furious with may not have the same feelings and thoughts of anger as you have. Unaware that they have caused any harm or hurt feelings, they continue to live their lives. You, on the other hand, continue to carry this hurt, anger and hatred within your body that not only disrupts your energy but also causes stress. Stress, produces cortisol, and high levels of cortisol can cause illnesses in the body years later. Forgiveness is not for the other person. When you forgive someone, it is a gift that you give yourself. Learn to let go of those hurts or reach out to the offender, express your feelings to them, and release the pain into the universe. In many religions, forgiveness is part of their teachings. Whether or not you follow a specific doctrine, forgiveness should be part of your life.

The Power of Prayer/Meditation

Meditation has been around for centuries and has been a ritual across the span of many religions. Some religions call it prayer while others, meditation. In some circles, meditation is a secular practice. Gabrielle Bernstein, author of *Spirit Junkie*, talks about how she was taught to meditate when she was 16 years old. As she got older, she let the practice go and found herself in a decade of addiction. She says that "when children have spiritual seeds planted in them, they know where to return." There is nothing outside of yourself that can bring you internal happiness. While the outside world can reflect what you feel on the inside, it can never bring you the peace and happiness you seek.

There are those who question the power of prayer and meditation and the healing effects on the body. Is the healing caused by God or is it the ability for the body and mind to heal itself through positive thoughts? Faith is the one thing that continues to baffle the medical community. There have been countless stories of terminally ill patients who, through strong and unwavering faith, made surprising turnarounds in their health. In many cases the patients went into remission or recovered. How can their miraculous healing be explained? I am not here to dispute the validity of God. I am here to remind you of the powerful force we have that can help us heal – whatever you call it, there is power behind it.

Consider the placebo effect- the idea that a person can show improvement in their health by the mere thought that they are getting medication when in actuality they were given sugar pills. Let us suppose you and I had the same illness. We went in for the same medication; however, you received the actual medication and I was given nothing but a sugar pill. Because I believe I have been administered the real medication, I feel positive that I am on my way to being cured. How could healing occur without the medication? What is it about my positive belief that allows the body to heal? Perhaps it is the comfort I have taking this "pill" which causes me to relax and to worry less thereby reducing my cortisol and stress levels. Because I have faith that this pill is working to fight my disease, my body is working towards healing. Some scientific evidence suggests that the placebo effect may be partly due to the release of *endorphins* in the brain. Endorphins are the body's natural pain killers. [16]

Dr. Herbert Benson, founder of the Mind/Body Institute at Harvard Medical Schools Beth Israel Deaconess Medical Center has said "Any condition that's caused or worsened by stress can be alleviated through meditation."[17]

A few benefits of meditation include:

- Lowered blood pressure
- Improved heart rate[18]
- Improved breathing
- Better memory and learning
- Reduction of PMS symptoms
- Improved fertility[19]

Dr. Christiane Northrup, author of Women's Bodies, Women's Wisdom believes meditation causes a reduction of cortisol and epinephrine while cooling the inflammation in the body.[20]

Whether you feel that it is mind over matter, prayer, or meditation, develop a practice that fits your spiritual life. Developing your own spirituality can increase your inner joy and improve your health.

"If you're feeling helpless, help someone." - Aung San Suu Kyi

CHAPTER 5

Career

What is my purpose?

W hen working in a job that does not use your talents, you may feel lost and directionless. Days seem long and you wait for the weekends. Each week, judging by the scores of social media entries, you are reminded about the drudgery of Monday. A few days later on Wednesday, you will find entries of people wishing each other a happy Hump Day, and a few days after that, TGIF (Thank God It's Friday) peppers your social media feed. Unhappiness causes stress on the body. Recently researchers in a Gallup poll found that 70% of Americans are unfulfilled and unhappy with their job.[21] Spending eight hours a day/forty hours per week/two hundred and fifty of the three hundred and sixty five days at work is a lot of time to be unhappy not doing what you were meant to do. You may work at a job because it provides you with what is needed to live – money. You need money to pay bills, for your retirement, and for your children but the manner in which you earn money leaves you feeling unsatisfied. You spend the weekend doing mundane chores and activities. By Sunday, you are struggling to sleep because you are dreading the new work week. Did you know that most heart attacks and other cardiovascular events occur on Mondays?[22] It is believed that these events can be attributed to work stress. In the 1990's there was a study of 683 patients, predominantly middle-aged men with implanted defibrillators and a history of life-threatening arrhythmias (irregular heart rhythms)[23]. The research showed a rise in arrhythmias on Monday. The reason was an overload of stress hormones such as cortisol and adrenaline.

According to Dr. Stephen Sinatra, an integrative cardiologist and author of the books *The Great Cholesterol Myth* and *Reverse Heart Disease Now*:

> *"What I find provocative about the study is that its participants showed a prominent peak in arrhythmias on Mondays—21 percent of episodes—even if they were no longer working! That was followed by a mid-week decline in arrhythmias and a second peak on Fridays. Not surprisingly, Saturdays and Sundays saw a 50 percent lower arrhythmia rate than did Mondays.*
>
> *Why do Mondays continue to be the peak day for arrhythmias? I believe that our bodies remember and anticipate stressful events. So, even though the participants in the study were not working, the fact that their bodies anticipated going to work on Monday triggered the identical biochemical stress hormones, increasing the heart attack risk factors that led to potentially lethal ventricular arrhythmias."*[24]

What steps can you take to minimize your risk of becoming a Monday statistic?

- Change your mindset. Remember the Law of Attraction states that what we focus on the most is what we attract more of in our lives.
- Make Sundays your day of rest and relaxation.
- Avoid strenuous exercise just before the start of Monday and give yourself a little extra commuting time to avoid the stress of rushing to work.
- Move a big meeting to another day of the week if you are in a position to control meeting times.
- Work from a place of passion. Find a job that matches your spirit.

When the majority of our time is spent at our jobs, wouldn't it be ideal if we were doing work we loved and enjoyed? If you do not know what you are passionate about or are not currently in a position to find your dream job, then try to approach your work as if it were your dream job. The energy you project is the very same energy that you will get back. Have you ever tried to deal with a difficult customer, coworker, or boss who is nasty or angry? If you respond in kind, the emotions escalate and the situation worsens. But if you respond with kindness, the difficult person may feel your calmness and have no choice but to give up their negativity. Do you remember the 1984 movie "The Karate Kid" with actors Ralph Macchio as Daniel, the Karate Kid and Pat Morita as his sensei, Mr. Miyagi? Mr. Miyagi projected very calm energy even in a fight. He never matched his opponent's energy but rather went with the punch. Like Mr. Miyagi, diffuse the negative situations in your office by reacting as a calm and positive energy. You will attract what you put your focus on.

My sister is a perfect example of the power of responding with calmness to a stressful work environment. There have been times when she has called me frustrated and angry about office politics or issues with co-workers. After allowing her a few minutes of venting, I would invite her to change the course of her day by considering the possibility that the co-worker may be having a bad day. Many times, she would tell me that by changing her negative energy to a positive one, the rest of her day turned out to be better and more pleasant.

Our current society tends to be "me" centered. We tend to focus our attention on how "I feel" or have a "what's in it for me" attitude. We forget one very important lesson – not everything is about us. When someone snaps at you or reacts in a way that may not be pleasant, be mindful that the underlying issue may have nothing to do with you. You may have done nothing to bring about that unpleasant event other than be the nearest person to lash out against. I used to take each snap or criticism personally until I heard this quote:

> *"Always remember that everything is not about YOU...*
> *sometimes a friend may act out of character because of something*
> *going on in their life that they may not want to share... they*

may not know how to express the confusion they are feeling...
this may be the very time they need your love more than ever
before... act with compassion and be the place of comfort for
them to come to for peace. A little bit of love will help them on
their journey." ~Karen Kostyla

That changed my life. While in some instances I may be at fault for a person's reaction to an email or something said, I no longer take every negative comment to heart. I think about what may be going in the other person's life. In no longer being quick to react to a negative comment, I find that my stress level has reduced. With this subtle change, your work environment can become a place you desire to go to every day.

Victoria Moran, the author of *Creating a Charmed Life*, talks about playing your "free square." She says that just as every Bingo player has a free square on their Bingo card, you, too, have a free square in your life. A free square refers to a talent or gift we each have – being a natural speaker, a people person, a great listener, a nurturer, or being naturally financially savvy. Knowing your natural talent is the key to having a "charmed life." If you do not know what your natural talent is, contact your best friend and ask him/her to tell you what they perceive it to be.

For many years I worked in a corporate environment. Now I am a business owner with a new set of challenges. One challenge that you as a business owner may face is working on tasks you find irksome and which cause you stress. You may avoid delegating those tasks for many reasons, one of which is a fear of letting go of control. The danger in not delegating is you soon find your work no longer brings you the pleasure it once had. The remedy is to let go of the things you dislike and focus on areas where your skill set is strongest and which make you happy. My "free square" is my ability to connect with others. I have been told many times that I am a great listener and I make people feel at ease. I most enjoy meeting with my clients and being outside the office. I am aware of my weaknesses: organization, administration, paperwork, and preparing proposals. I have been fortunate to have a fantastic support team whose talents are in the areas in which I am weak. Not every business owner enjoys being out in the field. Some are content with being behind the scenes. The key is to partner with or hire someone who can complement you. Delegating frees me to do the things I love and am good at.

My best friend, Patty, always had a gift for organization which dates back to when we were cadets at New York Military Academy. Yes, one would assume my five years attending military school would have instilled in me organization; however, despite the years of training, that skill never took. By contrast, Patty absolutely loves organizing. Often when we speak, she is organizing something – whether it is the cabinets, the drawers, or her closet. I have been telling her for years she can make a handsome living as a personal organizer as disorganized people like me would pay for her services. If she ever did work in that field, she would feel the joy that comes from having a sense of purpose. To her, it would never feel like work because she would be doing something that comes naturally to her.

About 4 years ago, my insurance industry was radically changing around me. I was questioning whether or not I still had the passion for my career. It was a trying time indeed as our commission payments were constantly being decreased even though our workload was ever increasing. I was slowly watching my client roster shrink because of competition from the government. It was a very difficult and trying time. I had to decide whether I was going to jump ship or learn to swim in these choppy waters. I took a moment to regroup and to think about how I could continue to add value for my clients while shifting into a new paradigm. I decided to test the waters with a new consulting service and fee schedule. I had never charged my clients fees as I had always been compensated by the insurance carriers whose products I sold. But as I dipped my toe in the "waters" of fee charging, I realized that my clients know the value I offer and were willing to pay me for my expertise. The passion for my career slowly reignited and I began to find it fun again as I enjoy finding solutions for my clients that make sense for them.

At the same time this was all occurring, I was also embarking on a new adjunct career in a field that I was passionate about – the field of nutrition. As far back as I can remember, I devoured books and magazines on different dietary theories. I remember as a young girl reading about the actress Jacklyn Smith and what she ate and how she exercised to look so beautiful. After reading her book, I began to read other books and magazines until one day a couple of years ago, my sister urged me to consider going to nutrition school. She was always calling me for advice for herself and her family and thought the field of nutrition was a perfect fit for me.

It would be a lie if I said I was not frightened by her suggestion. It almost felt like a betrayal of the career I had been in for 20 years. What would I possibly do with this schooling? Would I change careers at this stage in my life? Should I start a second business?

Within a couple of days of her suggestion, I enrolled in the Institute for Integrative Nutrition's Health Coach Program® (IIN). As I listened week after week to the lectures on my iPad, I realized how alive I felt, and I could not wait until the next lecture was available. Attending a couple of IIN's live annual conferences was an awesome experience. The conferences afforded me the opportunity to hear lectures from my idols like Deepak Chopra, Arianna Huffington, and Dr. Andrew Weil.

There is something to be said for looking at your hobbies to see what careers or businesses would cause you to work from a point of passion and happiness. When you work from a place of joy in what you do, success usually follows, and work rarely feels like work. My time at the IIN has been nothing short of wonderful. It is because of the connections I have made through IIN that I now blog for the Huffington Post and am working on so many creative projects.

You want to be in a job that is aligned with your spiritual being. Many jobs are diametrically opposed to who we are. For example, you may work for a corporation but you prefer to be a business owners. No one is saying to leave your job. Look for a work in a company that has a culture that speaks to who you are. An attorney friend worked for many years for a senior attorney who paid her very little in relation to her education and talents and created a work environment which dampened her spirits on a regular basis. Fear of not finding another position at another job kept her stagnant. Once she made the decision to search for another opportunity, she landed a position with a bigger firm for better pay that challenged her and lit up her soul. I saw the immediate change in her demeanor and in the way she spoke. I could see that while the new position was more demanding in hours, the work was very interesting to her, and she looked forward to each day.

Work from a place of abundance, not lack. Many people lose their jobs every year or are threatened by the possibility of a job loss. It is frightening when there are others who rely on your income. However, your mindset needs to come from one of abundance, not lack. Imagine if you were in a relationship where you stayed not because you loved your partner but rather because you thought there was no one else in the world who would love you. What if that partner came to you and said they wanted out of the relationship? How would you react? Would you be desperate to hold on to your partner even though you did not love him/her? If your friend were in that situation, what advice would you give? Conversely, if you knew that you could find love with another person and that you possessed the qualities of a good significant other, how would you react if your current partner wanted to break up? You would probably wish them good luck, get back out in the dating field, and would most likely find someone better suited. Living in a mindset of abundance attracts more positive people and things to you. Therefore, in the case of job loss, which is easier? Getting a new job when you are projecting energy of desperation or projecting energy of confidence that another job is just around the corner?

What keeps you from your dream career? It may be fear. Fear can be debilitating and prevent us from obtaining the very thing we desire. I was speaking with a woman who has many wonderful ideas but struggles with deciding on whether to look for a job in the industry she is comfortable with or pursuing an interest she has. She has great ideas for a business but is afraid to make the jump. Why is she hesitant to make the leap into entrepreneurship? Is it a fear of failure? Not knowing enough? What if nobody is interested in the services offered? Such fears keep her on the sidelines of life and prevent her from living a life from passion. If she takes a job for the sake of work, she will be once again on the hamster wheel she so wants to escape. How would other areas of her relationships, health or other Soul-Nourishing Food be affected? As I spoke with her, I could hear negativity in her voice. She is unhappy with the way her life is at the moment because of the battle raging between her heart and her head.

I understand that we all have money issues and sometimes taking a position for wages is needed to provide for our families, but if you have the ability to make a transition from a "job" to "fun" how different would life be? Would happiness permeate other areas of your life? We have to be authentic to ourselves and work from a place that builds on our strengths.

With everything you do, work from a position of pride, passion, and strength. Doing so creates a positive energy. Positivity will bring a sense of calm, less stress, more happiness and greater abundance in your life.

CHAPTER 6

Money

Friend or Foe

L et's talk about a touchy subject – Money. Do you view money as a friend or as a foe? You will never be able to change your financial circumstances until you change your mindset and feelings about money. Growing up you may have heard, "Money is the root of all evils," "You need money to grow money," "Money makes people do evil things," "You can never have enough money," "Money doesn't grow on trees," or "Having too much money is greedy."

Which of these statements remains with you today? Your inner beliefs about money may contradict your outward desires surrounding money. The goal is to align the inner and the outward so that you can achieve what you want. Spending habits such as over purchasing and hoarding may be related to an imbalance of other Soul-Nourishing Foods.

My Money Soul-Nourishing Food seemed off balance for a while. My spending habits were usually predicated on my emotional health. When I was lonely and bored, I would go shopping. I always felt the need to ensure I never ran out of an item. When I went shopping, I had to have multiples of the item or I would purchase something I may have forgotten I already had. This need to have enough had to do with my own issues of self-worth. Did I feel I was enough? Or was it because it was the only part of my life that I felt I had control over? A few years ago, I was laser-focused on my weight loss. I was working out regularly, journaling, and eating whole and unprocessed foods. I was happy in a relationship and feeling on top of the world. During this time my kitchen was neat and my refrigerator and cabinets were bare.

When my relationship ended, I was working through my grief. My exercise regimen came to a screeching halt, and in turn, my kitchen became cluttered while my refrigerator and cupboards began to burst with unnecessary food purchases. My state of mind was obvious by the state of my kitchen. Once I was able to recognize my chaotic kitchen was a reflection of my state of emotions, I was able to put a stop to the purchases. I vowed not to purchase another item (with the exception of perishables such as fresh produce) until I had used most items already in my cupboards. Shopping was my way of dealing with a painful situation. It was a way for me to feel in control, to avoid dealing with emotions. In hindsight, keeping up with my exercise regimen would have been a healthier, constructive, and more economical option.

Over-spending on food was not the only vice I used to help me deal with painful situations. In my 20s, I had moved to Boston for a position with a financial company. For a while, I was lonely and bored. I used to spend most of my free time window shopping. The window shopping regularly turned into a spending spree. I would purchase clothing on sale in a size I aimed to fit into, or I would purchase decorative housewares to spruce up my space. Shopping was a temporary means of happiness. During my time in Boston, I accumulated copious unnecessary things. After I moved back to my beloved Hoboken, NJ, my mother was preparing a trip to visit family in South America. I decided it was time to let go of the "stuff." Each unworn piece of clothing I pulled from my closet still had its original price tags. I filled two large suitcases of clothing in various sizes and styles and sent them to my cousins who were so grateful to have new clothes. The value of the clothing I had purged from my closet must have been easily over $1,000! To this day, thinking of how much money I would already have saved for retirement had I not spent money on frivolous items saddens me. I used money to fill the emotional void.

So much of our money is spent on items that do not nourish our souls but give us a temporary satisfaction. They are poor substitutes for what we are craving such as attention, love, status, validation, or companionship. Spending can be on anything that are wants but not needs. Needs are the things that are necessities to life such as the roof over your head, the clothing on your back, the food to nourish your body. Wants are things you desire but do not need to survive. The 3,000 square foot home is desirable but you could live comfortably in a nice cozy apartment. The 100th pair of shoes is great but not needed. I am sure you understand the concept. Spending more than you save will cause you to wonder how you live paycheck to paycheck. Prior to making a purchase, ask yourself some of these questions:

- Why am I going to shop for [fill in the blank]?
- What am I feeling or needing at this time and will this purchase fulfill that need?
- Is the purchase a need or a want?
- What will I lose out on if I spend money on something I don't need?
- Could I use this money to fund a dream vacation I always wanted?
- Could money be better spent on something that the kids have been asking for that in the past, something I never thought I could afford?
- Do I have enough saved for my retirement or do I want to continue working well past my retirement age?

Many times it is not a matter of taking on a second job or getting a raise. Sometimes it is a matter of budgeting and spending money on things that we need, not things that we want to use to fill a void.

David Bach, a financial planner and author of many books such as *Start Over, Finish Rich* wrote about the tiny expenditures we make each day without thinking about them. He coined a concept called The Latte Factor® since many of us are fans of expensive large coffee chain shops. If we were to calculate what we spend on our daily lattes, we would be very surprised at the annual cost of our designer coffee habits. Using his Latte Factor Calculator®, which can be found on his website, http://www.finishrich.com/free_resources/lattecalculator.php, I will illustrate how much money would be accumulated if we diverted the $10 spent on 2 lattes per day (one for morning, one for afternoon) and invested it in a financial instrument that produced a 6% annual return. Here are the results:

Number of Years	$10/day invested at 6% annually
1 Year	$3,869.00
10 Years	$50,996.50
20 Years	$142,323.45
30 Year	$305,876.12

If you were able to redirect your designer coffee budget and invest it, what would you do with that money? Save it for retirement? Take a vacation or a cruise to an exotic destination? Go to Disney with you kids? Put the money down on that car you need or want? Would $50,000 after 10 years be enough for a down payment on a second home or the home of your dreams? This is money saved just by forgoing designer coffee!

Now, let's examine how much money you would have if you kicked a nicotine habit. Currently, in NYC, a pack of cigarettes costs $13. Let's assume you were purchasing a pack a day.

Number of Years	$13/day invested at 6% annually
1 Year	$5,029.70
10 Years	$66,295.44
20 Years	$185,020.49
30 Years	$397,638.96

Wow! Now don't get me wrong, there are times when I like to splurge on a latte. I am not suggesting that we stop enjoying the little pleasures in life. Assuming you consumed both a daily latte and pack of cigarettes, after 10 years, you would have saved $117,292!! For some, the mortgage could be paid off in 10 years! That is mind-blowing. You can use David's Bach's calculator to find the value of any of the purchases you make regularly.

After reading one of David Bach's earlier books, *The Automatic Millionaire*, I decided to conduct an experiment. I went to a warehouse store, purchased a brand of coffee I enjoyed, and made my lattes at home every day. What I discovered was the average cost of my home brewed latte was $0.80 per day as opposed to the nearly $5 a cup at the big chain. That is a huge markup! And the coffee tasted every bit as good, if not better, because I had more disposable income left for the other things that mattered more to me such as taking a class or traveling. To this day, it irks me to purchase tea at these chains because I know at home, it costs $0.10 per teabag (not counting the cost of heating the water) while at the coffee shop it will cost me $2.45.

Budgets

Budgeting is an important tool used to curtail the small expenditures and to allocate money for the things that are considered to be "needs," and not "wants." Despite what you may think of when you hear the word budget, budgeting is a great way to help you see where your hard earned money is going and to make the adjustments necessary to reach your financial goals. A sample budget would list your total monthly household income minus all the expenses broken into monthly installments (i.e. rent, mortgage, auto insurance, food, childcare, tuition, school loans, utilities, clothing, and personal care).

There are three principles to budgeting:

1. Write down a goal or a dream and post it on your Vision Board (revisit subheading of vision boards in Chapter 1: Self Care/ Inner Joy.) Perhaps you have dreamt about owning a second home or saving $1,000,000 for retirement.
2. Write out your monthly budget. When you can account for every $1 spent, you are better able achieve your dreams.
3. Stick to the budget you have set for yourself and for your family.

A great tip to rein in spending is the use of envelopes. Mark each envelope with a category. Every month, insert cash in the monthly amount that has been allocated for that specific category. Let's assume you have a designated envelope for Happy Hours which contains $200 cash. Knowing that there is $200 in that envelope may make you think twice about that third cocktail or will motivate you to find less expensive options for a night out with friends.

Another tool is a pocket notebook or a mobile expense app. There are numerous budgeting software and apps available today. Sign up at www.tastingwellness.com to be notified when my app becomes available.

My aunt has a little pocket notebook in which she records every expense made each day. If she purchases a pack of gum she records it. Her commitment to her goals is astonishing. Keeping a record of her purchases made her more mindful. She and my uncle had a goal of owning a home in wine country. While they enjoyed life to the fullest during their working years, they saved enough to purchase a home in their desired location and to renovate the place over the years. Now they split their time between their country home and their apartment in the city. They travel regularly and have the financial freedom they dreamt about. You, too, can realize your dreams.

Check Your Credit

We are living in a time where identity theft is prevalent. It is very easy for others to open accounts in our name and ruin our ability to have good credit. Each year, we should check our credit reports to ensure that no unauthorized accounts have been opened, and that all information reported from our creditors to the reporting agencies is accurate. Any inaccuracies should be reported to the agency for them to correct. One year I ordered my credit report from one of the reporting agencies. The report read that I was married and named my brother-in-law as my husband. I immediately contacted the agency and informed them that I have never been married and wanted that misinformation removed as soon as possible. Having bad credit can cost you money in increased mortgage rates, higher insurance premiums, higher interest rates, or lower credit limits on your credit cards. When you apply for a job, employers will pull your credit report to see if you are a risk. In some cases, your dream job can be jeopardized by your poor credit.[25]

There is only one website that is sanctioned by the Federal government where you can obtain a free copy of your annual credit report from each of the three agencies – Experian®, Transunion®, and Equifax®. This website is www.annualcreditreport.com. I would recommend that you get the reports from all three agencies the first time you sign up. Then in subsequent years, order a report from one of the agencies at three different times per year. Doing so provides you a no cost way to make sure no unauthorized accounts or inaccuracies arise.

Wealth

What does wealth mean to you? Wealth and money are not synonymous. Definitions of wealth can differ among a group of people. For one person, financial wealth may mean having enough money to pay off the mortgage, to retire comfortably, or to have the means to care for aging parents. Another person's definition would be the ability to purchase, do, and achieve anything they want, whether to rent a private jet for a day excursion to Paris or to own a sports team. For yet another person, wealth may not equate to money but rather to a feeling of gratitude they have for the abundance of love, great health, and joy they feel each and every day.

Spend some time thinking about your personal definition of wealth and write it down in your journal. Be clear and detailed in your definition of wealth. It is not enough to write that you want a lot of money. Be clear on what that number is and give yourself realistic timelines on when you would like your goal to be achieved.

I hear so much from teenagers today that they want to be rich like the celebrities they see on reality TV shows. As I tell my niece and nephew, money does not define you. It does not mean that you are better than another person or that you have lived a better life. Having money may not bring you the happiness you are seeking. However, money does give you choices and a voice. Be wise about how you earn, spend, and save your money so that you live from a position of financial strength. When you are clear on what is most important, you may find that you may already be "wealthy."

CHAPTER 7

Enlightenment

Who Needs It?

T echnology has made our world smaller. We can communicate with family across the globe via video conferencing and cell phones. We can search for virtually any topic on the internet. With all the wonderful advances made with technology, we are doing less thinking. Do you remember having to memorize multiplication tables? How many telephone numbers could you remember? How many physical books have you read in the last year? Restaurant receipts now tell us how much the tip is based on a few percentages. Before the calculator and computer, we used our brains to do those calculations. With the advent of the cell phone, we no longer have to memorize telephone numbers as they are stored in our phones. Imagine what would happen if your cell phone was lost or dead while you were traveling in a remote part of the country and the only phone available was in a phone booth. Whose telephone number would you remember? Would you be able to call a loved one to get assistance? Luckily for me, my mother's telephone number is one digit different from my own, but I do not have my father's or my sister's numbers memorized.

Fewer people are reading physical books from cover to cover. The increase in television viewing is evident by the increase of the number of new channels being added to a cable subscription. Email newsletters containing snippets of information bombard our email in-boxes. There seems to be a reduction of attention span in our current culture. The news as well as other daytime shows keep their stories to just a couple of minutes per segment. Magazine articles are shorter and contain more bullet points, larger title fonts while the article titles are a synopsis of the following paragraph. These article features are known as a dual readership path in the blogging world. A dual readership path allows one reader to get the gist of the article by reading the title and skimming the page for key words or bullet points while another reader may read the article in its entirety. With a dependence on technology to calculate and memorize numbers, an increase in television viewing, and a shift in the way we listen to the news, have we dumbed ourselves down with technology?

Continual learning is vital to keeping our brains sharp and warding off diseases of the mind like Alzheimer disease and dementia. A 2002 Journal of the American Medical Association (JAMA) abstract cites a study of 801 older adults that shows how their frequent participation in cognitively stimulating activities is associated with reduced risk of Alzheimer Disease.[26]

Our brains contain neurons, a specialized cell whose job is to transmit information to other nerve cells, muscle, or gland cells. This intricate web of neurons resembles a complex wiring system. There are 100 billion neurons in our brains.[27] The communication between the neurons is what triggers our creativity and allows other thought processes to flow. When we stop learning or using our brains for various mental tasks, some of these neurons disconnect. Conversely, continual learning and sharpening of our mental skills creates new neurons to form and fuse with the other neurons. Dr. Daniel Amen, a neuroscientist and author of *Change Your Brain, Change Your Life* and *Making a Good Brain Great*, among others, says that the brain is like any other muscle in our body. When we stop exercising our brain, our mental "muscle" can begin to deteriorate. As little as 15 minutes a day of learning can prevent this deterioration from occurring.

There many ways of learning. Education can be formal or informal. There are many brilliant and successful people in society who do not have more than a high school education or who never graduated from college. When I refer to education, I am referring to your continual quest for knowledge. The topic can be centered on a favorite hobby such as photography, gardening, quilt making, or on a topic that piques your interest.

Expanding the mind is important in getting a broader perspective on life and to discover other areas you may never have realized would interest you. These new discoveries make life richer and fuller.

Have you ever been engrossed in a great novel that you spent the entire day reading? Were you eager to find out how the book ended because you felt transported by the storyline? There have been a handful of books that have been able to transport me for a short time and help me to forget about the stresses of the moment. Reading helps open the channel of creativity within us. As children, we were excited to listen to stories or to repeat everything we learned in a particular class. We were able to envision a world of endless possibilities. Some children dreamt of helping sick children and animals while others dreamt of traveling the world or eradicating an illness. However, as we grow up, we are influenced by societal ideas of how life should be lived and those childhood dreams are many times squashed to make room for ones not our own.

As adults, some of us may be fortunate to have followed our childhood dream path. Others may enter into professions our parents require of us or professions society convinced us would bring happiness. At the age of 40, I was finally taking classes I wished I had taken in college. You do not have to enroll in a formal program. You can look for informal, non-credit classes given at your local community college or online. You may attend lectures at museums or libraries. There are many wonderful, free online classes taught by professors from top universities available through Coursera. On sites like Eventbrite.com or Meetup.com you will find countless events and groups on a myriad of topics in which you may have an interest or did not know existed. Frequent your public library and borrow books and documentaries on DVD or CD on subjects that you have no knowledge about. If you are searching for a passion, this is a great way to start. You may stumble upon a new topic that ignites your interest. Consistent learning is not only good for your health, but also provides new topics of conversation, and keeps life interesting.

> *"Man's mind, once stretched by a new idea, never regains its original dimensions." -- Oliver Wendell Holmes*

CHAPTER 8

Home

Home Sweet Home

Your home can be a source of anxiety or a place of relaxation, and a safe haven after a long and stressful day at work. Maintaining a house that is organized truly helps with creativity. As mentioned throughout this book, good, positive energetic flow is necessary in various aspects of our lives to bring in more abundance. This positive energy is especially true in the case of your home. It does not matter whether you live in a mansion along the ocean or a little dorm room. What matters is that your space gives you the feeling of relaxation and tranquility regardless of its size.

How we maintain our home can be a sign of our state of mind. During my unhappy periods, my home would be messy and unorganized. As my happiness quotient began to rise, my home was neater and more inviting. Over time, I became better at organization. Having a pet helped me with organization as leaving things on the floor could harm her if she got a hold of a detrimental item.

Clutter can be a gauge on our emotional state. We may purchase unneeded items during periods of loneliness or boredom. Those items may be reflective of future desires such as losing weight or a learning a new sport. Letting go of items that no longer serve us may be difficult because of their sentimental value. Clutter can also be a reflection of our self-worth. In my home, the fullness of my refrigerator would be a reflection of my emotional state. During times of loneliness or boredom, I would over- purchase groceries and household supplies. The frequency and amount of shopping I did was something that I could control. Additionally, there is something about running out of supplies that makes me uncomfortable. Conversely, during periods of happiness and activity, my kitchen is low on supplies and virtually empty. Now when I see the kitchen overflowing with purchases, I take a moment to check my emotions and then course correct.

We are bombarded everyday with catalogues and junk mail. It is easy for paper to accumulate in our home if we do not discard it right away. One of the easiest things to do is to have a garbage can and a shredder nearby and as you get your mail, immediately throw out the outer envelopes, flyers, catalogues, and anything else that is not important. Shred all offers for credit cards and any other mail with your identifying information to avoid identity theft. With the remaining mail, either scan it into your computer, or have a little section where you have your mail stored. Every week, make sure to toss out or file all remaining invoices that have been paid. When you do not have piles of paper stacking up, it is easier to maintain order.

Whereas you may have an easy time discarding the unneeded papers, there are people all over the world with very serious hoarding issues. Hoarding is a very debilitating and heartbreaking mental illness. It is an obsessive compulsive disorder which causes those afflicted to have extreme difficulty parting with things regardless of their value. I am not referring to hoarding when I talk about clutter. If you feel you have a hoarding issue that has affected the safety and quality of your life and the lives of those you love, please contact a trained mental health professional to help you get to the root of your pain. Please go to Anxiety and Depression Association of America's website http://www.adaa.org/ for more information and to seek a trained professional.

Color

When I was growing up, my parents always changed something in their home every few years to breathe new life into the space. It could be through a change of paint color, new throw pillows, or a piece of furniture. While these changes were subtle, they subconsciously had a positive effect on our moods. Changing your home décor can give you a feeling of a fresh start. Dirty and chipped walls can make you feel depressed. A fresh coat of paint can make your space feel new again. Adding better lighting can improve your disposition especially on those cloudy days. There are times in life where things can begin to feel stagnant, and a few hours of a little redecorating in your home can produce a sense of renewal.

Painting the walls is relatively inexpensive. Invite your friends and family over for a painting party and the painting will be done very quickly. Don't be afraid of color. You may decide on painting one wall with a pop of color. This can add a little bit of drama to your space.

Adding color to your environment can have an effect on health. In ancient times, some cultures used colors to heal the body. The practice is called Chromotherapy but today it may be referred to as light therapy or colourology. Color can have an effect on your body. Have you ever noticed the color of the logos of various fast food signs? They are predominately yellow and red. These fast food giants have professionals who understand the psychology behind color. Red, yellow, and orange are stimulating colors which in combination trigger you to purchase and quickly exit the restaurant. These colors are not meant to entice you to stay and dine.[28] Some big chain coffeehouses will use green and other warm tones to invite you to stay and relax.

Understanding color psychology can help you achieve the desired feeling for a particular room. If you want your bedroom to be relaxing and conducive to sleep, perhaps reds, or yellows may not be suitable. Play with different colors and notice how they make you feel. The chart below can show you the therapeutic effects colors have on the body.

Color	**Therapeutic Use**
Red	Increase circulation, stimulate the senses/body, evokes passion/sex
Yellow	Purification of the body; nerve stimulation
Orange	Increase energy levels; heal lungs
Blue	Treat pain; sooth illnesses, produce calm

Green	Positively affects the functioning of the heart, lungs, and thymus[29]
Purple	Spirituality
Indigo	Alleviate skin problems

If you are renting, many times painting the walls is not allowed. There are many products on the market that can be used to decorate your walls such as removable wall decals or removable wall paper. These decals come in an assortment of designs and colors which can brighten up your space. You can also add splashes of color with home accents such as pillows, rugs, and curtains. Even bringing in a bouquet of fresh flowers can be a great cure for the white colored walls.

Besides adding color to your home, changing the placement of your furniture is an inexpensive way to change the environment. In Chinese culture, the placement of furniture was important to the energy within one's domicile. Feng Shui is one of the Five Arts of Chinese metaphysics which discusses the "invisible forces" that bind the universe, earth, and man together. Feng Shui, in the context of this chapter and as it is discussed in today's society, is the art and practice of arranging and decorating your home to produce a balanced and harmonious state energetically. One of the main tools used is a Bagua map. Feng Shui theorists believe that your home is broken into nine areas of life. A bagua map shows the placement of these nine areas. The areas of life resemble Soul-Nourishing Foods™. These nine areas on the bagua map are career, people, creativity, relationships, status, abundance, family, inner knowledge, and health & balance.[30]

What we have in these areas or how we have decorated them affects the energy of that specific area. For example, if you want more love and romance in your life, remove all pictures of solitary, lonely figures and replace them with pictures of happy pairs that reflect the love you want in your life. Everything in your room should be in pairs- two chairs, two pillows, two nightstands, two lamps, two water glasses. Your bed should be positioned away from the wall to allow each person to be able to access the bed from either side. If you are single and are looking for a mate, it would be advisable to clear out a couple of drawers and closet space in order to invite a person in. My father always told me to clear a space to invite love in. I recall a time when the man I was dating looked around my then cluttered home and wondered how he would fit into my condo if we were to move in together. Of course I told him I would make room, but I do not think he ever felt there was room in my life for him. Perhaps there was some level of truth in his feeling! Remember the saying "out with the old and in with the new!" When you free your home from clutter, you invite new things in. Your own energy should be one of love and positivity in order to attract a partner with the same energy.

If you want a more restful sleep, consider clearing out the storage under your bed and leaving that space empty. It is advised to remove mirrors from your bedroom as mirrors reflect energy which may affect your sleep.

If you have a home office and want new business, clear out the junk and the excess papers.

Open your windows often to bring in fresh air and let the natural light come in as much as possible. When I was looking for my current condo, the very first thing I noticed was the abundance of sunlight that came through the windows. I knew that this condo was the one for me. I always joke that I am like a flower – I thrive on sunlight. Moods can be greatly affected by the change in weather. Seasonal Affective disorder (SAD), is a depression that normally occurs in winter months, but can happen during other seasons, in response to changes in the natural day/night cycle. SAD affects millions of people especially in places that have long periods with a lack of sunshine. One of the treatments for this disorder is light therapy. Full Spectrum light bulbs have the ability to produce UVA and UVB rays in the same proportion as natural sunlight. Not all full spectrum light bulbs are the same.

Although there have been concern about these bulbs which contain mercury, according to Dr. Mercola, an alternative medicine proponent and osteopathic physician, unless the bulbs break, there should not be a health risk. He says that about 10 milligrams of mercury is needed per bulb as producing an LED bulb which contains no mercury would be very expensive.[31] A light box also contains full spectrum light and can help close the gap in the loss of daylight hours lost in the winter months.[32]

Plants

Plants are nature's mirror versions of our lungs. While our lungs work to bring oxygen in and expel carbon dioxide, plants take in carbon dioxide and release oxygen into the air. According to the results of a NASA clean air study[33], certain common indoor plants may provide a natural way of removing harmful chemicals such as formaldehyde, benzene, and trichloroethylene (TCE). Benzene is a colorless flammable liquid widely used in many common household items such as plastics, rubbers, detergents, dyes, drugs, pesticides and even in cigarettes. Benzene is carcinogenic and has been known to cause various types of cancer. [34] TCE is found in spot removing agents used in dry cleaning clothes, spray fixatives for hobby crafts and aerosol degreasers. In June 2014, the Environmental Protection Agency determined that TCE may harm our health and our environment.[35] It has been known as early as 1932 that TCE was toxic.[36]

With all the chemicals used in many items found in our home, it is important to bring in plants to cleanse and purify our air! Chrysanthemum morifolium is one plant that removes formaldehyde, benzene, and TCE as well as ammonia, xylene and toluene. For a chart of plants and the chemicals they remove from the air, visit http://en.wikipedia.org/wiki/List_of_air-filtering_plants.

The quality of air in our homes has a dramatic effect on our health and sense of well-being. Oxygen is the most important element we need to survive. During our local news programs, especially during the summer months, the meteorologist may discuss the Air Quality Index (AQI) rating for that day. The Air Quality Index advises the public on how clean or polluted the air is that day and what health effects may be experienced within a few hours or days after breathing polluted air. *"EPA calculates the AQI for five major air pollutants regulated by the Clean Air Act: ground-level ozone, particle pollution (also known as particulate matter), carbon monoxide, sulfur dioxide, and nitrogen dioxide. For each of these pollutants, EPA has established national air quality standards to protect public health. Ground-level ozone and airborne particles are the two pollutants that pose the greatest threat to human health in this country."* [37] The AQI has a range of 0-500 with 0 being the safest air quality and 500 being the most dangerous. The ranges are broken into 6 different levels of air quality with a different color associated with each level. For a comprehensive explanation and the AQI chart, please refer to www.airnow.gov and click on the link for Air Quality Index.

While air quality affects everyone, it is especially important for those with lung issues such as asthma, emphysema, and COPD for whom breathing may be more labored. Children and the elderly are also at risk. It is vital for us to create oxygen rich environments within our homes through the use of plants, maintaining a home free of dust and dirt, avoiding smoking cigarettes indoors, and regularly changing furnace air filters. Basic furnace filters are designed to trap dust, dirt, and airborne particulates before they can get into the system. More expensive filters have additional benefits in enhancing the air quality in your home by trapping bacteria, pollen, and mildew and mold spores. Since most of the air in your house circulates through your HVAC system, furnace filters are your first line of defense against dust and airborne allergens. How often should you change the filter? Check the owner's manual for the manufacturer's maintenance recommendations.

Non-toxic cleaners

If you are looking to improve the energy and the air quality in your home, it is important to be mindful of the types of cleaning agents you use. Harsh chemicals can harm your health. Have you ever read the back labels of some household cleaners? Some of the conventional products on the market have warning labels. On one popular product containing bleach that is used for removing mold and mildew in your shower, the label warns the consumer that its product is not recommended for use by persons with heart conditions or chronic respiratory problems. If inhaled, a person should move to fresh air. The product also may cause substantial skin irritation and temporary eye injury. Some popular window cleaners contain ammonia which can constrict your lungs causing difficulty in breathing.[38]

Remember that you, your children, and your pets are breathing these chemicals every time they are used to clean the house. There are many new non-toxic products in the marketplace that are effective cleaners without the dangerous chemicals. You can also make your own cleaning liquids with simple, healthy ingredients such as vinegar, water, essential oils, lemon juice, and baking powder. These homemade products are not only earth friendly but also safe around your children, and pets.

Many recipes for cleaners with various uses can be found on the internet. Experiment with these recipes. To infuse your home with a pleasant aroma, add a drop or two of your favorite essential oils to the cleaner you are making. Have fun while keeping your family safe, and keeping your home clean!

Enjoy your home. Let it be a place of safety, comfort and serenity for you and your family.

> *Don't save things for a special occasion. Every day of your life is a special occasion. – Thomas S. Monson*

CHAPTER 9

<hr>

Creativity

Finding Your Inner Child

<hr>

As children, we learn to draw, to paint, to play musical instruments, and to make macaroni art. We sing, we dance, we tell stories and we love the magic of movies. For most of us, as we age, our creativity goes into hibernation. We get wrapped up in the day-to-day activities that stifle creativity. As I mentioned earlier in this book, I was very creative as a young girl writing poetry, creating crossword puzzles, drawing and creating clothing for my Barbie doll. Later, as a young adult, I entered college and those endeavors were replaced with term papers and other classwork. After college, my time was spent in an industry that did not present many opportunities for artful creativity nor did I revisit those old hobbies until a couple of years ago.

Once I began to reenter the world of "art", I found that ideas began to flow more readily than they had previously. Drawing, writing, designing clothing, and trying other media such as cooking were liberating. There is a freedom that comes with self-expression. I felt more open to new ideas and became less rigid in my thinking.

My niece, Kat, is incredibly gifted in the area of creativity. From the time she was able to hold a crayon, she created such beautiful art work and wrote poetry that was beyond her years. When I was working on a title for this book, I asked her to read a few chapters. Within a few minutes, she had captured the essence of my writing in a thoughtful and fun title.

Many of us need to find our inner child - a time when stories colored our worlds through mental images and took us on mental journeys that brought us such delight.

Creativity taps into the inner child in each of us that seeks nurturing. We all need creative outlets such as reading, painting, cooking, wood working, journaling, writing, gardening, designing, inventing, or playing musical instruments. We may want to spend time in nature, museums, art galleries, and music venues — anywhere that sparks creativity.

Music

Have you ever noticed certain songs may take you back to a memory or feeling from the past? Music connects the human spirit and reminds us that we all share the same emotions and trials and tribulations. Our souls are intertwined through the power of music. We have all experienced heartbreak, loss, devastation, joy, love, and happiness. These emotions are our common thread even though the circumstances or the stories may differ in their detail.

Those "ear worms," songs that get stuck in our heads, tend to be the ones that reflect the dominant feeling we are having at that moment. When I was 16 years old, I would torture my freshly wounded and broken heart by endlessly listening to 80's ballads and other songs of heartbreak. Like so many teenage girls, I would lock myself in the room and cry over the loss of a relationship. Today, I know that if I continue to listen to those types of songs, as beautiful as they are, I will spiral into a depression. Therefore, I am very careful not to listen to more than one or two songs of that genre. Instead, I try to find those upbeat "anthems" that lift up my spirits. When I want to clean the house or run on the treadmill, I make sure to have hours of dance music to motivate me.

For centuries music has been used for healing. Consider the Shamans who used music for healing by putting the subject into a hypnotic state. Chanting in Hindu and other cultures is used to open the mind, lift the spirit and heal the body. Today, music therapy "is an established health profession in which music is used within a therapeutic relationship to address physical, emotional, cognitive, and social needs of individuals."[39] According to the *American Journal of Public Health*, music therapy has been shown to decrease anxiety and has been used "as a strategy for achieving control over pain."[40] In addition to anxiety reduction in an individual, it can also improve immune system function. Music therapy is even covered under most medical insurance policies if it is considered medically necessary.

In one study, forty-five patients who had suffered heart attacks were observed to see the effects music had on their conditions. They were broken into three groups. One group was assigned twenty minutes of music in a quiet and restful environment. The other two groups did not have music therapy. The study showed that the group assigned music in a restful setting experienced immediate reductions in their heart rate, myocardial oxygen demands, and respiratory rates. Even after an hour, these reductions remained significantly greater.[41]

Dancing

Related to music is dancing. Last winter, I was invited to a dance studio grand opening. It is owned by three Dancing with the Stars® pros. They offered every attendee a trial dance lesson with one of their dance instructors, so I decided to go and take a formal dancing lesson. The mere thought of dancing made me uneasy. I used to love social dancing when I was younger. It had been so long since I danced, and the first and last ballroom dance class I took was not much fun. Remembering the phrase "get comfortable with being uncomfortable," I decided to practice getting out of my comfort zone. I partook in the introductory ballroom dance class and discovered that I enjoyed it very much. Immediately following the introductory class, I made the decision to sign up for the smallest package the dance studio offered. The following Tuesday, I returned for my private class, followed by a group class, and then a social. I loved every minute of the three hours that I was dancing. It did not matter whether I knew the steps or the proper hold. What mattered was that, for three short hours I was able to express myself through dance and feel a freedom within my body that I had not felt in a very long time.

Dancing, as with other movement- based creative expression, has been shown to increase body image, quality of life, and better range of motion.[42] Dancing has also been shown to offer a 76% reduced risk of dementia! [43] It may be a good time to put on your dancing shoes!

Journaling and Other Forms of Written Expression

Many people are not emotionally open. They may be embarrassed, may not feel comfortable sharing their emotions with others, or may not have someone to confide in. Bottling up emotions can cause more stress related visits to the doctor, a greater absenteeism from work due to depression, and in children, lower grade point averages.[44] Writing for just 15-20 minutes a day can greatly improve one's health and mental wellbeing. Some long term benefits of writing include improved mood,[45] and better asthma management[46]. The act of writing about stressful events and the emotions felt may help a person purge these feelings. It may also give the person a different perspective on a situation once they see it in writing. Catharsis may lower a person's blood pressure, and lower stress levels which in turn improves the functioning of the immune system.[47] If something as simple and inexpensive as expressive writing can have such a profound effect on your health, could you write a few minutes a day?

Julia Cameron, the author of *The Artist's Way*, introduces her readers to her concept of morning pages. Julia writes, "Put simply, morning pages are three pages of longhand writing, strictly stream-of-thought consciousness. Morning pages are the primary tool of creative recovery."[48] Do not censor your thoughts or feelings. Feel free to add in a few expletives. Your morning pages can comprise of brooding, joyful, childish thoughts. These pages are for you to write about anything and everything that is stuck on your mind. You may write about needing to do the laundry, hating your boss, or feeling frustrated with your spouse. There is no right or wrong way to complete this exercise. It is akin to the diaries we kept as kids. We may have written that we hated our mother, our sister, our father or some stupid chore we were ordered to complete. We may not have meant these words to be literal, but writing them made us feel better. Since these morning pages are for your eyes only, I suggest that you shred and discard them immediately after writing. With your mind constantly racing, morning pages help rid the brain drain. When you clear your mind of the clutter, you invite creativity and new thoughts to flood in. Discarding the mental clutter is also a symbol that those thoughts are no longer needed.

Other forms of Creativity

Being creative does not mean you need to become an artist or a musician. Creativity can flow in the way you perform everyday activities. Most of us are creatures of habit. You may have a set morning routine in which you brush your teeth in the exact same pattern. Breakfast may be comprised of the same foods each day. You may dress yourself in the same order where socks go on before you put on your pants. Aim to change these routines by perhaps brushing your teeth or hair with your non-dominant hand, or put on your pants followed by your socks. Instead of eating a bagel every day for breakfast, try eating eggs, vegetables, or even fish for breakfast. Send a creative email or text message to someone you love. Drink tea instead of your regular coffee.

My nephew's seventeenth birthday just passed and I had not yet purchased a card for him. As I was reorganizing my closet, I came across an album of pictures of him when he was two years old. There was one of him and me that I loved. I decided to make him a card using that photo. After making a copy of the photo on my printer, I pasted the photo to a decorative piece of paper and wrote a message inside. At his party, I gave him a gift which contained the card inside. My nephew loved the card and it became a central part of the evening.

Creativity can be demonstrated through fashion. Stylists and makeup artists demonstrate to women how to be creative with their hair and makeup. Men may show their creativity with their hair and with their ties or socks. A friend of mine loves to wear crazy looking socks with his conservative suits. He posts daily pictures of his socks on his social media.

The other day I was walking my dog. Making the decision to be more present on our walks, I had decided to leave the cellphone at home. On one block I stopped to notice a plant with leaves that were nearly three times the width of my foot. It seemed to have been there for a while however, this was the first time I noticed it. There have been streets I have traveled down regularly and still find something new to discover. Next time you drive or walk down a familiar road, pay attention to various details and see if you find something you have never noticed before. Being curious about your surroundings is a form of creativity.

The more you are present, experimental, and engaging, the more your creativity will begin to flow. Through this process, you may find new interests to keep you busy.

> *"An essential aspect of creativity is not*
> *being afraid to fail." -Edwin Land*

CHAPTER 10

Health

What's Wrong with Me, Doc?

As I have mentioned in previous chapters, for years my celiac disease was misdiagnosed until I took charge of my own health. I never gave up the exhausting search for answers. While there are many highly competent doctors, they are human and do not have all the answers. In addition, many allopathic physicians -those doctors who combat disease by use of prescription medication or by performing surgery- have very little knowledge about nutrition. Allopathic medicine is the mainstream medical care in the United States.

In a 2010 national survey of 127 accredited U.S. medical schools, only 26 required a dedicated nutrition course. Overall, medical students received 19.6 contact hours on nutrition during their medical school careers (down from 22.3 hours in 2004).[49] Additionally, pharmaceutical companies have influence over medical school curriculum. In 2009, a Times magazine article reported,

> *"Of Harvard's 8,900 professors and lecturers, 1,600 admit that either they or a family member has had some kind of business link to drug companies — sometimes worth hundreds of thousands of dollars — that could bias their teaching or research. Additionally, pharmaceutical companies contributed more than $11.5 million to the school last year for research and continuing-education classes."[50]*

Many medical conditions do not have a pharmaceutical remedy. Celiac disease is one of them. This is most unfortunate because had there been a pharmaceutical drug for this condition, I would have been diagnosed decades before. On the very day I decided to give up on allopathic medical doctors and find out on my own what had been ailing me, I had just visited a highly recommended allergist. He performed various allergy tests and informed me there was nothing wrong. He took out his prescription pad and wrote me a prescription for an EpiPen. After I left his office frustrated and upset to have received yet another unnecessary prescription, I went to the book store and pulled every book off the shelf on food allergies. I sat in a comfortable arm chair and began to read. In one book, I read of a woman experiencing the same symptoms I had. Reading her story made me cry because it was in that moment that I discovered I have a gluten allergy. A few months later I saw a celiac disease specialist who confirmed that I have celiac disease. I felt so let down by the traditional medical community. Why didn't the allergist know about celiac disease? Why did so many doctors tell me my symptoms were all in my mind? Since that fateful day, I have seen this allergist on popular television shows speaking as an expert on celiac disease!

Celiac disease is not a new disease. It affects 1% of Americans, approximately 3 million people.[51] Additionally, as many as 18 million Americans may have non-celiac gluten sensitivity (NCGS)! With approximately 300 symptoms associated with celiac disease, it's no wonder why this disease is not better diagnosed.[52][53]

Celiac disease and gluten sensitivity cannot be managed with a pharmaceutical medication. The only way to manage celiac disease is through a change of diet – namely eliminating wheat, barley and rye from one's diet.

When I began having symptoms of thyroid and hormone changes, my doctors told me it was nothing. Again, I began to research to figure out what was happening to my body. I was eating a healthy diet, getting proper exercise and yet, I had symptoms of fatigue, hair loss, brain fog, and low libido. From my research, I had deduced that I was perimenopausal. My OB/GYN argued that it was impossible for me to be in perimenopause due to my age, but I reminded her of its possibility due to my autoimmune disease. She decided to take a blood sample and the lab test results revealed that I was indeed in perimenopause. Once again, I was right in my assumption. After some more research, I sought out an endocrinologist who put me on bio identical hormones as we had agreed upon. After a few months, the symptoms were not improving as much as we anticipated. When I spoke with my doctor about my concerns, she told me "You'll never feel more than 50% better." Her statement shocked me as I thought to myself that I am too young to go through life feeling 50%. That was when I made the decision to go outside the allopathic medical community and find a naturopathic doctor who knows the world of alternative health.

According to the American Association of Naturopathic Physicians, *"A licensed naturopathic physician (ND) attends a four-year, graduate-level naturopathic medical school and is educated in all of the same basic sciences as an MD, but also studies holistic and nontoxic approaches to therapy with a strong emphasis on disease prevention and optimizing wellness. In addition to a standard medical curriculum, the naturopathic physician also studies clinical nutrition, homeopathic medicine, botanical medicine, psychology, and counseling. A naturopathic physician takes rigorous professional board exams so that he or she may be licensed by a state or jurisdiction as a primary care general practice physician."* [54]

Currently, only 17 states license Naturopathic Doctors (ND). The remaining states limit the scope of practice and do not allow NDs to diagnose and treat conditions. Therefore, Naturopathic Doctors, in the states that do not license NDs, need to make sure every patient seen also works with a conventional doctor to have physical exams and laboratory test prescriptions. It is my opinion that the American Medical Association (AMA) has lobbyists in various states preventing naturopathic physicians from being recognized as primary care physicians. In the states that do not license NDs, the services of naturopathic physicians are not covered by medical insurance.

For a comparison of the education between allopathic and naturopathic physicians, go to http://www.nyanp.org/find-a-naturopathic-medicine-new-york/naturopathic-doctors-education-comparison-other-doctors/.

Fortunately, I have been working with a naturopathic doctor (ND) whose has made me feel "normal" again. She has helped me through dietary changes, exercise, and nutritional supplements. How is my ND able to help where other doctors failed? My ND sat with me and reviewed my entire medical history beginning from my birth. She worked tirelessly to get to the root of my symptoms. In doing so, she was better able to help my body heal. Natural healing is not a quick process, but it is worth the journey.

I wanted my mother to see the ND for her own medical issues but she was reluctant. She was used to allopathic physicians. I brought her with me to my doctor visits as an observer in the hope that she would feel more comfortable with the process. As she began to see the wonderful and positive changes in me, she made an appointment for herself. She has been feeling the best she has ever felt in her life.

My story is not to bash the allopathic medical community, but rather to remind you not to accept mediocrity when it comes to your health. No one knows your body better that you do. What is normal for one person may not be normal for you. There are many wonderful advances in modern medicine. Allopathic medicine is the right solution for many acute situations. I have seen the wonders of allopathic medicine at work. Allopathic medicine is good at managing symptoms, but I feel naturopathic medicine works at getting to the root cause of medical issues. Not everything is solved with prescription medications that may cause multiple serious side effects.

The message I want to impart is to be your own health advocate and an advocate for those you love. Do not accept a diagnosis without going for a second and/or third opinion. If you are still not better, do not give up searching for an answer. Trust in your intuition. Do your research.

Complementary and Alternative Medicine (CAM)

Complementary medicine is a term that refers to a group of diagnostic and therapeutic disciplines that are used parallel to or in tandem with conventional medicine practiced in the West. For example, a homeopathic remedy, such as Arnica pellets, may be given to a patient after surgery to lessen bruising and pain.

Alternative medicine is those practices such as naturopathic medicine that replace conventional medical practices. (As you may recall in previous chapters, I mention that I now see a Naturopathic Doctor as opposed to an allopathic one.)

Complementary and alternative medicine are not taught in Western schools or used in traditional medical settings. While many other countries have adopted complementary medicine into mainstream medicine, the United States still lags behind.

There are a number of CAM offerings which I will not discuss in great detail in this book. My intention is to open your mind to other treatment possibilities. Here is a list of a few included under CAM:

- acupuncture
- Alexander technique
- aromatherapy
- Ayurvedic medicine
- biofeedback
- chiropractic medicine
- Craniosacral therapy
- diet therapy
- herbalism
- holistic nursing
- homeopathy
- hypnosis
- massage therapy
- meditation
- music therapy
- naturopathy
- nutritional therapy
- osteopathic manipulative therapy (OMT)
- Psych-K
- Qi gong
- reflexology
- Reiki

- spiritual healing
- Tai Chi
- traditional Chinese Medicine (TCM)
- yoga

If you are not getting the results you want in the form of treatment you are currently receiving, give one of these CAM practices a try.

Food Plans

Just as there is no one right way to treat a medical condition, there is no one-size-fits-all when it comes to food plans. What may work for one person may harm another. You may thrive on a vegetarian diet, yet your friend may develop a thyroid condition and feel lethargic as a result of being vegetarian. It is important to find a lifestyle that works for you.

In my quest to help the cause against animal cruelty, I attempted to become a vegan. Vegans do not eat any animal protein. I have a number of friends who have been practicing veganism for years and thrived. Unfortunately for me, soon after embarking on the vegan diet, I felt lethargic, suffered from brain fog, and was frequently hungry. I began to add animal protein to my meals and felt better as a result. Later, after I met my naturopathic doctor, she guided me to embark on a Paleo diet. The Paleo Diet is based on the foods eaten by humans during the Paleolithic Era namely, animal protein, vegetables, some fruit, nuts and seeds. Humans did not eat grains. In looking at my blood work, my ND noticed that my body did not process carbohydrates in the form of grains and in turn caused inflammation in my body. Grains are a big part of a vegan diet. Removal of grains from my diet was not easy at first, but doing so has made a tremendous difference in the way I feel and in lowering the inflammation in my body.

There are books on over a hundred dietary theories available in the marketplace. You can research them at your local library, find books at a bookstore, or work with a Certified Integrative Nutrition Health Coach such as my classmates who graduated from the Institute for Integrative Nutrition® who can help find a plan that best works for you and your body. Be sure that the professional you choose has studied various theories and is not a sales representative from a supplement company disguised as a "health coach."

Sleep

We all know the importance of enough sleep, yet many of us are severely deficient in this area. Sleep deprivation is common amongst many new parents and medical residents. Additionally, as we age and our hormones levels begin to change, our sleep patterns will change as well. The amount of sleep needed is unique to the individual. However, not getting enough or good quality sleep produces a sleep debt we can never repay no matter how much catching up we do. Too little sleep can affect our mood and productivity. Sleep deprivation can be deadly.

Prior to 2011, it was not uncommon for first year medical residents to work shifts that lasted longer than 30 hours. While the argument for them working such hours was to gain experience, human errors and lapses in judgments increased when fatigue set in. Imagine getting behind the wheel after being awake for 30 hours? When my cousin was a medical resident, she suffered through these long shifts. There were many times she was so exhausted that she would call someone to pick her up rather than attempt to drive home. I recall hearing a story about her fellow resident who was in a serious car crash because of sleep deprivation. Luckily, she did not injure anyone and survived the accident.

After much heated debate, in 2011 a new rule was enacted requiring that first year residents work no longer than 16 hour shifts. Second and third year residents are allowed to work up to 28 hours but cannot take on a new patient in the last four hours of their shift.[55]

For new parents, there is no law in effect limiting their parental duties. In two parent households, a couple may agree to take turns getting up when the baby cries for a feeding or diaper change. Single parents may not have that luxury. In this case, grabbing any amount of sleep whether in consecutive hours or broken into a series of naps is needed.

Sleep is necessary for our bodies to replenish cells. It aids in decreasing appetite and reduces the risk of diabetes and cardiovascular problems. Additionally, it reduces the risk of depression, substance abuse and increases cognitive abilities such as reflexes, concentration, and memorization. Your risk of falling asleep at the wheel or making a fatal mistake is greatly reduced when you have had 7 to 9 hours of sleep daily. If you are frequently fatigued, aim to get to bed a little earlier. Start with getting to bed 15 minutes earlier and gradually increase the time so that you are getting into bed with enough time to give your body the sleep it needs.

Daytime naps can be helpful for those who are sleep deprived or for those who need a little rest. For those who can nap and still be able to get a good night's sleep later in the evening, there are many wonderful health benefits. A twenty minutes nap can increase alertness and motor learning skills. A nap lasting thirty to ninety minutes can increase memory, and human growth hormones, which are responsible for repairing muscles and slowing down the aging process.[56] [57]

For those with sleep issues, try using the morning pages or journaling rituals discussed in Chapter 1: Self-Care/Inner Joy. Sometimes all that is needed is to write down all the chatter that is running through our heads. Keep a piece of paper and a pen next to your bed so that every time a thought pops up that you need to remember, you can write it down. The act of writing down your thoughts will reduce stress and anxiety.

Another tool to ease you into healthful sleep is to create a sleep ritual. An hour before bed, terminate use of all electronic devices and begin preparations for sleep. Some preparations may include, washing your face, flossing and brushing your teeth, taking a hot shower or bath, or reading a book. Turn on relaxing music, practice easy and relaxing yoga poses, or do some deep breathing exercises in bed.

Limit or eliminate your use of caffeine and alcohol. Contrary to popular belief, both are stimulants. When alcohol is first consumed it is a stimulant but after sometime in the body it may have a sedating effect. The reason why alcohol should not be used as a sleep aid is because it increases the frequency of waking, thereby reducing the amount of time spent in REM sleep, which is the most important and restorative phase of sleep.[58] Upon awakening, you may feel fatigued even though you have slept eight hours.[59]

Sex is also a great sleep aid as a hormone called prolactin is released after orgasm. This hormone is responsible for the feelings of sleepiness and relaxation. Engage in safe sex often as there are many other health benefits to this activity.

Getting the right quality of sleep is important. Try some of the tips I provided or find ones that work for you.

Vacation

In the United States, there are no statutory laws requiring that employees get paid vacation time. In Europe, employees receive twenty days of paid vacation and in Japan, employees get ten. Not only do employees outside of the US get paid time off, but they also get anywhere from five to fifteen paid holidays.[60]

People who take vacations have lower levels of stress, and have more motivation to attain goals. They are more creative and happier. In turn, they have lower levels of stress and a reduced heart disease risk. If you are part of the population who does not receive paid vacations, aim to take at least one day off every other month and plan an overnight trip somewhere relaxing and fun. A change of scenery is always great for the spirit.

Taking care of your health is not just about popping pills or seeing doctors. It is about taking care of our bodies and our spirits.

CHAPTER 11

Movement

No Couch Potatoes, Please

W e all know that moving our bodies through some form of exercise is necessary for good health. Although this comes as no surprise, we are not getting enough activity each day. Unlike our ancestors, many of us have desk jobs at which we are inactive for six to eight hours per day. The commute to and from work is usually by automobile or by mass transit. After work, we may sit in front of a television to unwind. Movement is necessary to keep our bodies limber and our joints lubricated. The benefits of movement are to keep the body from being stiff, send blood flow to our brains, and strengthen the immune system. The key to physical activity is to find activities that continue to engage and interest us long-term. For some of us, the movement of choice may be a group sport such as an adult soccer or basketball team. Others may prefer dance classes or yoga.

Prolonged sitting can be lethal. Sitting more than six hours per day can reduce a man's life expectancy by twenty percent while for women, the reduction of life expectancy is forty percent.[61] Lack of movement is detrimental not only to our bodies but to our brains. Dr. Daniel Amen, a psychiatrist, brain disorder specialist and author of over 30 books including *Change Your Brain, Change Your Life*, believes that lack of exercise is detrimental for our brain health. "Exercise boosts blood flow to the brain, which helps supply oxygen, glucose, and nutrients and takes away toxic substances."[62] This healthy blood flow to the deep areas of our brain helps with our coordination and processing of complex thoughts. Exercise assists in slowing the aging process and creates new brain cells that we need for memory and judgment.[63] While exercise, in general, nourishes the brain, activities that elevate heart rate and require coordination such as tennis, dancing or aerobics are best for enhancing thinking and processing speed.

For many years, I was a couch potato sitting in front of the television with a tub of chemically-laden, artery-clogging ice cream, and a bag of greasy potato chips. Every muscle, tendon and joint hurt when I attempted the slightest amount of walking. Getting off the couch was not easy, and I felt fatigued all the time. However, I learned that it is during times of fatigue that I need to move to gain energy. A body in motion stays in motion! When you are feeling tired, the best cures for fatigue are to get up off the couch, move, and drink a glass of water. Often fatigue comes from being dehydrated.[64] After a few minutes, you will begin to feel more energized.

Walking is a great form of exercise. Depending on the speed and intensity of movement, it can be cardiovascular in nature and will get the blood circulating in your body. If possible, leave your car parked and walk to your destinations. If you live in a rural area, walk in the woods. In general and depending on how fast you move, a mile will take you 20 minutes or less on foot. Not only are there many health benefits to walking, but you can also save on gas as well as the wear and tear on your car.

Many of my friends and family get frustrated when they visit me, as I refuse to drive to a restaurant or to the movie house if it is within walking distance. The City of Hoboken, NJ, is a mile square with very limited parking, so it makes sense to walk everywhere. Not only is it small but it is located on the other side of the Hudson River from NYC which can be accessed by train, bus, ferry or car. When I need to see clients in NYC, I walk to the Hoboken train station and head into the city by train. Once in NYC, depending on time, I walk to a client's offices without taking a connecting train or bus. Additionally, I have an energetic dog who also enjoys walking and reminds me to take her out when I am home. When time allows, she will accompany me on my 4 mile walks. All this activity is how I am able to get in up to 5 miles of walking a day.

The ability to walk five miles did not happen overnight. I began walking slowly for twenty minutes which equated to less than a mile at my initial slow speed. Over time, I progressed to the five miles at a moderate pace. Sometimes I walk the five miles at one time and other times the distance is accumulated throughout the day. Find what works for you. Most experts will recommend getting in ten thousand steps per day. Depending on your stride, ten thousand steps is about four miles. Invest in a pedometer or activity tracking device. These devices have mobile apps which may track your activity, the intensity of an activity, number of stairs climbed, and even your sleep pattern. These devices can be highly motivating to those of you who respond to goals and validation. My activity tracking device will send me a mobile phone notification alerting me if I am close to or have exceeded a particular daily goal.

There are many fun forms of exercise in which you can engage. The key to a lifelong commitment to exercise is to find a physical activity you really enjoy and to remember that movement should become a daily habit akin to teeth brushing.

In *Chapter 13: Dual Energies*, I discuss the masculine and feminine energies that are within each of us. These energies have nothing to do with our gender or sexual orientation. Different exercises enhance different energies within us. If you have a dominant masculine energy and need to enhance the feminine energy within you or vice versa, a healthy mix of activities will help bring you back into balance. For example, competitive sports, weightlifting, Iron Man competitions, kickboxing, Cross Fit, or running, may attract those with dominant masculine energies, while yoga, ballet, swimming, or stretching would be a good idea to bring in a healthy dose of feminine energy. Having a healthy balance of both can be instrumental in maintaining harmony in your body.

Strength Training

Strength Training is an important component to aging gracefully. Strength training refers to resistance exercises that increase strength and endurance. These resistance exercises can be completed with a set of dumbbells (free weights), machines, or body weight. Strength training does not mean that you becoming a competitive weight lifter with bulky muscles. Many benefits to strength training aside from a toned body include reduction of bone loss, protection against joint damage, a boost in your metabolism, an increase in certain important hormones, and an increase in libido. If you are new to strength training, seek the help of a Certified Personal Trainer (CPT) to teach you the basic positions to avoid injury. You can hire a trainer for one or two individual sessions for the basics or ongoing sessions to keep you accountable and motivated. Some CPTs have reduced pricing for group sessions. It is important to find a trainer you really like working with; otherwise, you will not stick with the program.

If you cannot afford a trainer, your local gym membership may include several complimentary personal training sessions. There are also a number of workout videos you can stream through Netflix, YouTube, or your current cable package. Lastly, look at the videos available through your local library.

Balance Training

I am of the firm belief that everyone should do balance exercises daily. As we age, our balance and coordination decrease. Working on balance will provide you with the stability you need to avoid unnecessary falls which may lead to unwarranted trips to the emergency room. I have tripped many times on the many uneven sidewalks around town, but what has kept me from falling is my ability to balance and position my body to regain a better footing. I owe my balance to yoga. There are balance exercises everyone can do in just a few minutes a day.

My friend, Lisa E. Picek, BS, CPT, has created a few balance exercises for you. Lisa is a Certified Personal Trainer and Functional Movement Specialist. She has trained high ranking military personnel as well as high level executives of large financial institutions. In addition to the exercises below, she and I are working on a workout program which will be released soon. Go to www.tastingwellness.com and subscribe to be notified via email when the program is released.

As with any exercise, it is important to begin slowly to avoid injury. Therefore, in week one, select one exercise to do each day. Do ten repetitions of the exercise on each leg. The exercise should take no more than five minutes to complete. In the following weeks add one more exercise so that by the end of week four, you are doing each of the four balance exercises routinely. The total time for all four exercises should be approximately fifteen minutes.

Balance Exercise One: Step Up

The step-up is a great beginner exercise to develop single-leg balance and aid in the strengthening stabilizers of the core.

Tools Required: A step, a step stool, a solid crate, or a treadmill. In choosing, select a step that is no more than knee height. The thigh should be parallel to the floor when foot is placed on step. Note that if a step is too high it can cause knee issues.

- Stand facing squarely to the step keeping your back upright and spine neutral
- Begin by placing your whole foot flat on the step
- Hinging at the hip, ascend by fully extending the lead leg
- Do not allow the opposite leg to touch the step
- Descend leading with the opposite leg continuing to focus on the hinging of the hip
- Keep lead foot on the step through the entire set

Balance Exercise Two: Lateral Hurdle Step-Over

The lateral hurdle step-over is the perfect beginner exercise for strength and agility. It will strengthen the adductor and abductor muscles as well as hip flexors.

Tools Required: Towel

- Create a hurdle by rolling up a towel and placing it on the floor to your side
- Arms can relax at sides or be placed behind head for more of a challenge
- Begin by lifting your leg closest to the towel so that your knee is at about hip level

- Step over the hurdle, leaving space for the following leg
- Lean slightly from the hip as the other leg follows and steps beside first leg
- Repeat, switching sides

Balance Exercise Three: Self-Assisted Single Leg Squat

The self-assisted single leg squat targets the quadriceps while utilizing the dynamic stabilizers of the hamstrings and calf muscles.
Tools Required: A sturdy wall

- Place hand on a prop or wall that is a sturdy structure for support
- Begin by standing on one leg and wrap the opposite leg around the back placing the toe on the ground to the outside of the foot
- Knee should point in same direction as your foot
- Squat down by bending your knee forward and pushing your hips backward
- Focus on keeping a neutral spine and back straight
- Descend until thigh is parallel to floor
- Return to stand focusing on utilizing the least amount of resistance from the wall as necessary
- Return and repeat. Continue set utilizing other leg

Balance Exercise Four: Single Leg Deadlift

The single-leg deadlift strengthens a chain of muscles including the hamstrings, adductor magnus, and gluteus muscles. Because the exercise is performed on one leg, less weight is required putting less stress on the back. This exercise also aids in the development of dynamic flexibility of the hamstring muscles.
Tools Required: A light dumbbell (5-10 pounds for beginners) or a full water bottle.

- Begin in a single leg stance
- Hold a light dumbbell in opposite hand of supporting leg
- Keep back straight, core tight, and shoulder blades retracted downward

- Begin by lowering the upper body hinging at the hip
- Movement begins at the hip
- Focus on keeping back straight, and keeping a neutral spine
- Slide the dumbbell along the thigh and shin of the supporting leg
- Push your hips backward and bend knee slightly while hinging
- Return to start and repeat through entire set

After the end of four weeks, you will begin to notice that your legs are stronger and going up stairs is easier.

Types of Physical Activity

There are the staples such as walking, stair climbing, running, yoga, swimming, strength training, but there are so many other activities that are equally as fun. I want to list them to illustrate the many activities that keep you moving without feeling like chores. These include:

- Rock Climbing
- Parasailing
- Trail hiking
- Martial arts – Judo, Muay Thai, Karate, Mixed Martial Arts (MMA)
- Ballet
- Wrestling
- Cycling
- Boxing
- Gymnastics
- Trampoline jumping
- Trapeze classes
- Zumba
- Dancing, ballroom or other
- Jumping Rope
- Fencing
- Tennis

- Adult community sports leagues such as soccer, lacrosse, dodgeball, baseball, football, rugby, softball
- Rowing
- Skateboarding
- Rollerblading
- House Cleaning and Yard work
- Canoeing, paddle boarding, surfing
- Skiing and cross country skiing
- Wii videos
- Playing hop scotch and tag with your children

The list is endless, and I am sure you will find a number of activities that will inspire and motivate you to move your body. Choose one or a few of them to maintain variety. Try an activity that you have not done before. You may be surprised to find your inner child emerge, your energy level increase, and your smile return.

CHAPTER 12

Home Cuisine

Feeding Your Body Gluten Free

W hy would home cuisine be considered a Soul-Nourishing Food™? The reason is that what we eat has a profound effect on health and mood. For those of you who do not have an issue with gluten, continue reading this chapter for I discuss other benefits of home cuisine.

My Path to Health

I suffered my whole life from digestive issues that were misdiagnosed. Some doctors dismissed me telling me that my symptoms were all in my head. Others were not skilled enough to make a proper diagnosis. I spent years trying to figure out the cause of my symptoms which ranged from severe fatigue to blisters on my face and body. After meeting with an allergist, who was the tenth or so doctor who advised me that there was nothing wrong, I walked straight to my local bookstore to find books that would help me understand what was happening to me that no doctor could do. As I sat in one of the comfortable armchairs with a stack of books on food allergies, I found my story on the pages of one of those books. I cried because I knew I was not crazy. I had finally found a long awaited answer to my suffering. I learned that what I was eating made me very sick, and it was called gluten. Gluten is the protein in wheat, barley and rye that gives elasticity to your favorite breads and croissants. For millions of people with celiac disease, an autoimmune disorder, the protein cannot be processed in the body, as the body triggers an immune response in the small intestine. This reaction causes inflammation that damages the small intestine's lining and prevents absorption of nutrients. If you continue to eat gluten, you will have intestinal damage which eventually will cause vital parts of your body to be deprived of necessary nourishment. For some people, the inflammation may lead to intestinal cancer. Celiac disease is an incurable, genetic disease that may lie dormant for many years. The disease may be triggered by environmental, physical or emotional events.[65] [66]

After reading the book that described celiac disease, I went on a modified gluten-free diet (I say modified, because at the time I did not know that gluten is prevalent in many products including some ice creams) and immediately began to feel a little better. I made an appointment with Dr. Peter Green, head of the Celiac Disease Center at Columbia University. The earliest appointment I was able to obtain was four months out. During one occurrence of ingesting gluten which caused facial swelling accompanied by a severe blister outbreak, I snapped a picture. When I met with Dr. Green, I shared my story with him and showed him the picture of the outbreak. Upon seeing the picture, he proclaimed, "You have Dermatitis Herpetiformis!" "Herpeti what?" I thought to myself. He explained to me that a small percentage of people with celiac disease also get painful and itchy blisters on the body. I was overjoyed to finally meet with a doctor with answers. After a few tests to confirm what he already knew, he explained that celiac disease is genetic and that I had been suffering from the disease for most of my life. My official diagnosis was made in May 2011. It was the beginning of a very interesting, yet liberating journey for me.

This chapter is titled Home Cooking, so how does this relate to my discovery that I have celiac disease? After my official diagnosis, I attended seminars led by Dr. Peter Green and his center's nutritionist who spoke about gluten free diets and how to navigate the minefields when eating out and grocery shopping. I was amazed by the myriad of products that contained wheat. I began to doubt that there was anything safe for me. The more I read on the topic, the more I began to notice the correlation between gluten and approximately 300 symptoms that may be attributed to gluten.[67]

For those with celiac disease and gluten sensitivity, there is no cure or magic pill. Managing celiac disease while dining out is not as simple as requesting gluten free dishes. There is the issue of cross contamination. If a restaurant does not have dedicated equipment, there is a risk of the food being contaminated with even the smallest amount of gluten. Imagine you are at your favorite Italian restaurant which does not have a dedicated kitchen. You innocently order a salad assuming there are no gluten ingredients in the salad. In the same kitchen, the chefs are also making pizza dough. Flour is floating in the air from the tossing, stretching, and the rolling out of the pizza dough. This floating flour lands on everything in the kitchen. The chef handling dough is wearing the same gloves used to make the pizza and is touching everything for your dish from the plate to the salad ingredients. You eat the salad thinking it is safe and then later wonder why you are experiencing symptoms. The amount of gluten it takes to cause harm to someone with gluten sensitivity or celiac disease can be as little as a piece of cracker the size of 1/8 of your thumbnail. That miniscule piece will have a prolonged inflammatory effect in the body for up to six months after ingestion![68]

I have been to a pizza parlor with friends, had only a glass of water, and still managed to become very sick. How? Because flour is airborne and is everywhere – the table, the glasses, the water, the napkins. And if my hands are touching these contaminated items and I accidently touch my mouth, there is a great chance these specks of gluten will enter my body when I lick my lips.

What is someone with a gluten sensitivity or Celiac disease to do? Home cooking is the answer. There are a handful of restaurants with gluten free awareness training certifications and dedicated gluten free kitchens. However, most meals I eat are prepared at home in my kitchen. Everyone who visits knows that I do not allow any foods containing gluten to enter my home. My home is the only place where I can have peace of mind and feel safe in managing my disease.

Initially, at diagnosis, I believed celiac disease was a curse. It felt that way during my transition into gluten free living. Today, I believe having celiac disease has been a blessing. It has forced me to cook at home, thereby controlling what I put in my body. How many times have you looked at food labels and read the ingredient lists? If you did, you would be surprised how many products from salad dressings to ice cream contain a form of gluten. Additionally, you would not recognize many of the chemical additives used to make a food product.

There are so many fantastic books on the subject of celiac disease and gluten sensitivity. Go to my website, Tasting Wellness (www.tastingwellness.com) for a list of books and other resources to learn more about this disease.

Toxins in Our Foods

Knowing what is in your food can greatly affect your health. Is your produce organic? Is your beef grass-fed? Is the milk you and your family consume organic and hormone and antibiotic free? The antibiotics and pesticides found in our food supply can be detrimental to your health.

Many conventional farmers use pesticides to control insect infestation. You may also be using pesticides on your lawn and home garden. The United States Environmental Protection Agency states on their website, "Laboratory studies show that pesticides can cause health problems, such as birth defects, nerve damage, cancer, and other effects that might occur over a long period of time. However, these effects depend on how toxic the pesticide is and how much of it is consumed. Some pesticides also pose unique health risks to children."[69] The pesticides can block essential nutrients necessary for their growth. If the child's excretory system is not working properly to flush out toxins, the toxins may begin to build up in his/her body. Pesticides may cause permanent altering of the manner in which their biological system operates![70]

The best way to reduce the amount of these pesticides entering your body and the bodies of your family is by growing and purchasing organic produce when possible. At the current time, organic produce is more expensive than conventionally grown produce. The prices for organic food will eventually come down when we all continue to request and require more organic produce in our stores. We vote everyday with our wallets by what we purchase. While I would prefer you to purchase all your fruits and vegetables from organic farms, below is a list of those that should be purchased organic as they contain the highest amount of pesticides.

- Apples
- Strawberries
- Grapes
- Celery
- Peaches
- Spinach
- Sweet bell peppers
- Nectarines (imported)
- Cucumbers
- Cherry tomatoes
- Snap peas (imported)
- Potatoes
- Hot peppers★
- Blueberries (domestic)★

★ May contain organophosphate insecticides, which are "highly toxic" and of special concern. Organophosphate attacks the nervous system in the same way that sarin, a nerve agent, does.[71]

Even milk may not be as healthy as we were taught to believe. The controversy about milk's health benefits keeps growing as more and more health experts speak out about the dangers of cow's milk. One health expert, Dr. Mark Hyman, author of books like *Blood Sugar Solution* and *UltraSimple Diet*, says, "Dairy contains some very allergenic proteins, such as casein, which can be problematic for many people. And to make matters worse, the casein that's in our modern dairy -- sourced from modern, hybridized cows -- has been genetically altered, creating a much higher likelihood of inflammation, autoimmune disease, and even Type 1 diabetes."

Another health expert, Dr. Joel Fuhrman, who authored *Eat to Live* and *The End of Dieting* has said, "Cow's milk is the perfect food for the rapidly growing calf, but foods that promote rapid growth promote cancer."

I wanted to learn more about this controversy, which is why I decided to sit down with Tatiana Barrera, author of the book *No Milk Please*, and the author of my book's Foreword. She, like her mentors, believes that dairy consumption may affect numerous people. Avoiding dairy is not only about those who are lactose intolerant; a high percentage of us lack the ability to produce the enzyme lactase needed to process and breakdown lactose, even if we have never been diagnosed with a lactose intolerance per se. She is very clear in her book that everyone's body is different and that there is not a "one size fits all" eating plan but rather a bio-individual approach.

With that being said, the milk that our ancestors drank was raw, unpasteurized, and from cows that roamed freely, received sunshine regularly, and ate grass that was not treated with fertilizers. There was no 1 percent, 2 percent or skim milk. Most of the milk produced today comes from cows that are confined to tight quarters, fed hormones and antibiotics, and die early from over milking.

In the early 1970s, a hypothesis was developed by Dr. Kurt A. Oster. He believed that when homogenization became the standard practice in the US back in the 1930s and 1940s, the incidence of atherosclerosis heart disease began to climb. He theorized that homogenization of milk increased the biological availability of xanthine oxidase (XO), an enzyme that has the capacity to oxidize or change plasmalogen, "a substantial part of the membranes surrounding the heart muscle cells and the cells that make up the walls of arteries."

Have you been experiencing a little depression, mild mood swings or feeling pain? Mild depression was something that I suffered from regularly until I removed dairy products from my diet. When I ingest dairy, a day or two later, I begin to suffer depression again. Why? Because when your body does not have the enzymes to process the lactose, the undigested particles travel through your intestines into your blood stream. The body sees these undigested particles as foreign invaders and sends an immune response in the form of inflammation. The immune response is the body protecting itself.

We've all seen the ads with celebrities sporting milk mustaches and touting milk as healthy. Most people drink milk for the protein, calcium and the satiety that it provides. But there are many other foods that have protein and calcium. Additionally, these foods such as spinach, kale, and nuts to name a few, provide satiety. These foods are more alkaline than acidic. What does that mean? Foods such as milk, meats, processed foods, and sugar change the pH in our body and cause acidity. Then there are foods like lemons, fruits and vegetables that can make us more alkaline. When we are taking in a higher ratio of acidic to alkalinizing foods, we are at risk for disease to manifest. The school of thought is to take in a 2:1 ratio of alkaline to acidic foods each day to keep disease at bay.

Tatiana believes that eliminating milk totally is not necessarily the answer, but to consider it as unhealthy as soda. It is "a matter of changing our cultural way of viewing it." Tatiana says we may be flexible and not necessarily avoid milk completely but have it in moderation. So what are we to drink in place of cow's milk? She adds it is not to replace milk with "milk" but to find an alternative like water. Water is a healthier beverage alternative as it is best for growing healthy cells. With all the other beverages we consume that are either caffeinated or laden with sugar, we are often dehydrating our bodies and not replenishing the much needed water in our cells. Water is needed for healthy brains, organs, skin, and hair, as well as to flush out toxins.

If you still want to enjoy your favorite latte or foods sans dairy, you may consider alternative "milks." There are a number of alternative "milk" options readily available in your local supermarket and health food stores such as soy, almond, coconut, hemp, and rice milks. As always, make sure the alternative milk you purchase is free of genetically-modified organisms (GMO) and some thickening agents. Making your own nut milk is very easy.

Visit www.tastingwellness.com for a quick and easy nut "milk" recipe.

Remember, total elimination of milk from our diets may not be required, but rather an understanding that milk should be consumed in moderation. For some, totally eliminating milk may reduce pain and depression and produce greater happiness.

Cook with Love

You may have heard people say about their cooking that "It was made with love." Does the intention of love have any effect on our food? According to a study published in the Journal of Science and Healing, a placebo-controlled trial was conducted among 62 participants to ascertain whether or not the focused intention enhances the beneficial effects of chocolate. After a week of the trial, the study concluded "The mood-elevating properties of chocolate can be enhanced with intention."[72]

The energy with which you cook influences your food. Before you cook, take a moment to notice what you are feeling at that moment. Is it frustration, exhaustion, anger, or sadness? Take a moment to acknowledge your feelings. Cry or scream if needed to release the negative energy from your body. Cook when you are in a more positive state.

My mother is a gifted cook. On several occasions, I recall her telling me, "I have no desire to cook" or "I am so bored of cooking." It was on those occasions that the meal was not as tasty as the times where she prepared food from a space of love. Whether cooking for yourself or others, always cook from a place of love and gratitude. Take nothing for granted. Make a ritual out of your cooking time. Light a candle to add a little bit of spirituality to the cooking, put on some uplifting music, and pour yourself a little beverage in your favorite glass. Through the warm energy you send to the food you have prepared, you may change the mood of those you love.

Smaller dinnerware

American culture is of the belief that bigger is better – bigger cars, bigger dinner entrees, Big Macs, Double Whoppers, Super Gulps are just some examples. A dinner entree at many restaurants has enough food to feed two to three people. Americans believe that if a dinner entree is not big enough, they are not getting their money's worth. Yet in Europe, almost everything is smaller. The serving sizes there are what used to be "normal" in our country.

In the *Journal of Nutrition,* "According to Nestle, this trend began in the U.S. as early as the 1970s, with portion sizes increasing sharply in the 1980s and continuing to rise. The growth of portion sizes has been most evident in fast food restaurants where the "supersizing" of some menu items is relatively common. Items available at fast food restaurants are estimated to be two to five times larger than two decades ago." [73]

Dinner plate sizes have also increased over the last century. According to a *Forbes* article from 2012, *"How Size and Color of Plates and Tablecloths Trick Us into Eating Too Much"*, Professors Brian Wansink and Koert van Ittersum "...found that the average size of the American manufactured dinner plate has increased by almost 23% from 1900. They also noted that plates were just over 9 inches in 1900, around 10 inches in 1950 and creeping towards 12 inches in 2012."[74] It is no wonder that obesity rates have climbed over that time period! It is time that we went back to the smaller plates so that we shrink our waists. A standard coffee mug now holds 16 ounces of liquid, and I am having difficulty finding 8 ounce coffee mugs. In my uncle's house in Paris, his wine glasses hold about an 8 ounce serving of wine while here in the states most red wine glasses can hold up to half a bottle! During their recent visit from Poland, I offered my guests coffee which they accepted. When I pulled out the coffee mugs, they could not believe the size. They were the standard 16 ounce mugs that come in a table setting. As I poured the coffee, they asked that I fill it only halfway. This happened again when my family from France stayed with me.

Recently, the government proposed a change to food labels. One of the changes was to change the serving sizes to reflect the true amounts people eat today. For example, a standard pint of ice cream has 4 servings at 1/2 cup per serving. But under the new labeling, a pint of ice cream is now listed to have 2 servings at 1 cup per serving.

The point is to be cognizant of how much you are serving yourself. There is no need to fill your dinner plate completely, knowing that the plate can hold two or more servings. Consider using a salad plate instead of a standard dinner plate. When you are attempting to reduce your food intake, plating food on a smaller plate will look fuller than plating the same amount of food on a larger plate. You will feel more satisfied after eating from the plate that looks more voluminous.

Home cooking is not only a matter of being gluten free but also knowing what is in your food, the quality of the foods, and the intention with which you nourish your body and the bodies of those you love.

CHAPTER 13

Dual Energies

The Fine Dance between Masculine & Feminine

By now, most of us have heard of *The Secret*, a movie and book that came out about a decade ago discussing the Law of Attraction, one of the seven laws of the universe. The basic premise of the Law of Attraction is that we attract whatever we focus our thoughts on whether good or bad. According to this Hermetic philosophy of Ancient Egypt and Ancient Greece, that dates back over 5,000 years, everything in our universe is governed by these laws. Another one of the seven laws is the Law of Gender. The Law of Gender states gender is present in everything. The idea that we all have masculine and feminine energies within ourselves is not a new concept. These dual energies have nothing to do with gender or sexual preference. There are masculine and feminine energies all around us in nature. According to the book *The Kybalion,* based on the mystical teachings of Hermes Trismegistus, the law of gender states that "gender is in everything; everything has its masculine and feminine principals; gender manifests on all planes." The masculine and feminine energies are not only found in humans but in electrons, plants, minerals and magnetic poles.

Let me give you my short history to better explain this duality. I was raised to be a strong female at a time when my generation was riding the coattails of all those women who paved the way for female equality. My father believed in the education of females and in raising empowered women who could stand on their own two feet without the need or necessity of a man. I have always been entrepreneurial and self-reliant in a male-dominated industry. Throughout my life, I have nurtured and overdeveloped the masculine energy that fuels this type of success.

Masculine energy is action-oriented, to the point, competitive, cognitive, direct, entrepreneurial, problem solving, and risk taking. These are some of the dominant traits found in entrepreneurs, CEOs, and other leaders who typically take charge and love to achieve goals. Conversely, feminine energy is rooted in intuition, receptivity, collaboration, creativity and feelings, to name a few. Make no mistake. Feminine energy is not submissive nor is it weak. At a time when women are in the workforce and running businesses, we are leading with our masculine energy. We are not developing or nurturing our feminine energy in order for us to find balance in our lives and in our relationships. Can you relate to this?

Have you ever felt misunderstood or been told you are too aggressive, too emotional or too much of another specific trait? It may be that your dual energies are out of balance. Once you begin to balance your masculine and feminine energies, you will find a freedom within you that you have never found before. As I have discovered, the process of balancing them is a process worth taking.

I began to explore this concept to determine the role it played within my romantic life and how to strengthen my underdeveloped feminine energy. Many times, I have been told by male friends that I was too "Type A" -- a term they used to refer to masculine energy dominance.

Besides reading on the topic, I began taking ballroom dance lessons to strengthen my feminine energy. In ballroom dance, there is a leader who is usually the male (masculine energy) and a follower, a female (feminine energy). During my first few classes, my instructor would request that I stop leading and anticipating the next steps, and allow him to lead. A good dance leader is one who can guide his dance partner through touch and sight. A follower can feel the direction and the steps by the energy and the touch of her partner. By giving up my "control," I was better able to follow his lead which led to a more enjoyable and pleasant dancing experience. Dancing became easier when we were not competing against each other (masculine energy) but rather working as a team (feminine energy). The result of letting go, trusting and receiving his gift of safety was freeing and allowed me to enjoy the experience.

One of my good friends is in the middle of a divorce from his wife. He has been having difficulty understanding why his marriage is ending. We discussed what it was about his wife that attracted her to him. He said he loved her ambition for her career. As they began to have children, they decided that she would remain home to care for them. As time progressed, her career ambition faded. While she is a great mother, he began to miss the traits she had when they first met. During this same period, my friend suffered from depression which hampered his ability to reach his full potential. Money began to be a central focus of their disputes. As time progressed, they were both dominant in their feminine energies. One of them needed to be in a dominant masculine energy and the other in a dominant feminine energy to be synergistic.

The Law of Polarity, is another of the seven laws of the universe that discusses opposites in life such as hot/cold, light/dark, negative/positive, and feminine/masculine. When my friend and his wife were both in their dominant feminine, it was only natural that one of them balance out the energy by stepping into his or her dominant masculine. When circumstances in their lives changed, she returned to the workforce to run her father's business. It was at this time, she asked for a divorce. Why? Because she was not happy being in her dominant masculine energy. She preferred her feminine energy and wanted him to step into a more masculine, energetic position. It was within his masculine energy that she felt the safest. Not knowing how to verbalize what she wanted or needed led to more frustration and a severing of their union. Once I explained to him the masculine and feminine energetic roles and how they played into their relationship, he was better able to understand his role in the demise. It is my hope that with this new understanding, perhaps he can rekindle what they once had when they first met.

As previously mentioned, I have dominant masculine energy. However, I have been finding that, with the shift of energies, my male friends have been responding to me differently. I have changed the way that I write my emails from a direct and to-the-point approach to a manner that is softer and differently worded. I am still able to get my point across and be effective while balancing my dual energies. The change is apparent in how they respond and react to me. One male friend said that my feminine side is one he preferred because I was freer, laughed more, and showed a more vulnerable side. When my masculine energy is dominant, it is like having a protective shield around me. Perhaps, subconsciously, I am protecting myself through my energy.

In Part II of this book, I list some exercises to help you balance out your energies. It is my hope that with a healthy balance of your masculine and feminine energies, you will have better relationships and find greater happiness.

Your task is not to seek for love, but merely to seek and find all the barriers within yourself that you have built against it. - Rumi, 13th Century Poet

PART II

13 Weeks to Balance and Happiness

Exercises

Practice

We all expect fast results. I am no exception to wanting a quick fix to happiness. However, life can be very long so you want to work on being happy over the course of your time on this earth. With each little step you take to make positive changes in each of your Soul-Nourishing Foods™, over time those little steps will compound. When you attempt to do too much too soon, it can become overwhelming. It's like trying to climb a ladder too many rungs at a time. You may fall down quicker. The best thing to do is to go slowly as this is a lifelong practice. One day, you will catch yourself smiling for no reason and that smile will be filled with a contentment you have never felt before. It will be at that point that you will recognize that your smile and feeling of contentment is your inner joy.

On the following pages are various ideas to help you strengthen each of your Soul-Nourishing Foods. Each week, select three options in one Soul-Nourishing Food category and practice them over the week. For example, in week one your Soul-Nourishing Food category is Self-Care/Inner Joy and your three selected options to practice are 1) bath ritual, 2) using the nice glasses, and 3) meditation.

The following week, choose three options from a new Soul-Nourishing Food to work on while continuing to practice one of the three exercises from the previous week.

For example, in week two, for Socialization you have selected to three practice exercises, AND selected to continue the bath ritual your previous week of Self Care/Inner Joy.

In week three, you continue the bath ritual (Self Care/Inner Joy) and meeting with friends (Socialization), and then add a three new exercises from Soul-Nourishing Food number three.

At the end of week 13, you should be practicing one exercise from each of the 13 Soul-Nourishing Foods to improve balance in your life. You are free to repeat the 13 week cycle as many times as you need to reach a place in your life where you feel more balanced. Keep in mind that life balance is a lifelong practice. However, as you feel happier and learn to take better care of yourself, handling life's ups and downs will be easier and getting back in sync will go more smoothly.

I caution you to not aim for perfection as life is never perfect.

Soul-Nourishing Food One: Self-Care/Inner Joy

- Upgrade your vegetables – try a new one each week.
- Give yourself little pleasures such as sitting outside and sipping your favorite beverage, watching the sunrise/sunset, laughing with your friends. Life is all about the little pleasures that we gloss over every day during our quest for the bigger ones.
- Drink good quality coffee and tea. Consume good quality chocolate and food.
- Plate your food as a restaurant does.
- Use actual plates that are not made of paper or plastic.
- Utilize your nice glasses.
- Set the table and add some flowers and candles. Dim the lights and have some soothing music.
- Give yourself the best.
- Buy yourself an assortment of something you enjoy such as tea or lingerie. Choose to drink, or wear, the one that suits your mood. There is something fun and empowering about having choices.
- Forgive yourself.
- Dr. Weill's 4-7-8 Breath exercises – When stressed, slowly take in a deep breath over four counts, hold for seven counts and release over eight counts
- Bathing rituals – bath beads, bath salts, bubbles, soap in a fragrance you love, or hair care you prefer.
- Meditate.
- Exercise.
- Write your morning pages.
- Fuel your body right.
- Treat yourself as someone who matters.

- Find a new restaurant.
- Call up a friend and see how you can help them.
- Get a manicure and pedicure.
- Get your hair cut/colored/styled.
- Wash you face and remove makeup before bed.
- Floss and brush your teeth nightly.
- Perform oil pulling. Oil pulling is an ancient Ayurvedic practice of taking extra virgin sesame seed or coconut oil in your mouth and swishing it for anywhere from 5-20 minutes. The theory is that the oil and saliva help pull toxins from your body. Do not swallow any of the oil as it has toxins pulled from your body. Spit it into the garbage as to not clog and damage your pipes in your house.
- If you are anxiety prone, avoid watching news programs for prolonged periods of time. Yes, we should be aware of what is happening in our world, however, the media sensationalizes a lot of stories. One hour of news is an hour of negativity and sadness which will cause more anxiety and stress.

Soul-Nourishing Food Two: Socialization

- Leave the cell phone in your car's glove compartment or turn it off for an hour or two and really connect with the person sitting across from you.
- Schedule time to meet with your friends.
- Go on Meetup.com and find a group that interests you. If you do not see a group that speaks to your interests, start one.
- Call a friend or family member you have not spoken to in a while.
- Join a sports league or travel group.
- Organize a sports league or travel group if one is not available in your area.
- Reciprocate invitations.
- Avoid jealousy or competition. Instead, share in your friend's good fortune.
- Practice active listening. This means really paying attention to what another person is saying without distractions.
- Avoid oversharing. Remember, your friends are not your therapists.
- Show appreciation. Thank your friends and let them know how much they mean to you.
- Make a new acquaintance.
- Cultivate a sense of humor.
- Be a positive light to others. If someone is negative, lift them up with positivity.
- Avoid the "misery loves company" crowd. Be an example through your actions.
- Read a book on social skills.

- Smile when in public. Smiling disarms people and changes the flow of energy.
- Host a movie or game night at your home.
- Maintain a neat home so you will be more open to having guests.
- Volunteer at a pet shelter.
- Volunteer for to be a Big Brother/Big Sister. Go to www.bbbs.org for more information.
- Volunteer at a senior center and share conversations with its residents.
- Ask your company if you can bring your pet to work.
- Get your pet certified as a therapy dog.
- Reconnect with childhood friends.
- Re-establish old friendships.
- Seek therapy to mend old wounds that are impediments to your social life.
- Share your feelings with your friends. Being a little vulnerable strengthens connections.

Soul-Nourishing Food
Three: Relationships

- Choose to project love in order to receive it.
- Make time for fun with your partner.
- Practice being vulnerable with someone you love.
- Hug for 10 – 20 seconds.
- Hold hands with your partner.
- Give or receive a massage.
- Engage in regular kissing.
- Practice mind-body therapies like yoga or breathing exercises.
- Take ballroom dance or other type of dancing that makes you feel sexy. It's important to get in touch with your sensuality.
- Leave your partner little notes of love in various places that they would look.
- Send your partner text messages of appreciation or something a little more risqué to let them know they are on your mind.
- Send emails of appreciation to your friends to let them know how much you value their friendship.

Soul-Nourishing Food Four: Spirituality

- Serve others — Sometimes the best remedy to our feeling of despair and sadness is to reach out to someone you know and ask them how you can be of service. Helping others redirects your attention, brings a sense of accomplishment and help make life better for others.
- Volunteer — instead of helping those you know, reach out into your community and offer to help make the lives of strangers a little better. Some places to consider are homeless shelters, nursing homes, adult day care centers, cancer centers in local hospitals, or animal shelters. Go to sites such as VolunteerMatch. org or VolunteerGuide.org for other options.
- Become a Big Brother Big Sister — go to www.bbbs.org for more information.
- Direct your energy towards positive thoughts. You will receive more of the thing you put the most focus on whether good or bad. If you catch yourself thinking a negative thoughts, turn that thought into a positive statement.
- Be one with Gratitude — take a few minutes a day to reflect on the little things that bring you a feeling of gratitude.
- Attend various denominational services to find which service aligns with your beliefs.
- Commune in nature. Take a trip out in nature and really observe your surroundings.

Soul-Nourishing Food Five: Career

- Think about your natural talents. Is it making people laugh, listening, speaking, or writing? If you do not know, ask your friends and family to give you a list of your best qualities.
- Network, network, network. Join a networking club, or frequent various business events. When you network, you increase your circle of contacts.
- Take a class to help you become more marketable in your profession or desired profession.
- Take a course on negotiation and selling. Whether you realize it or not, you are selling, and negotiating on a regular basis at work, at home, and in everyday life.
- Update your resume regularly
- Keep track of all your accomplishments no matter whether big or small. Write them down. When you are feeling blue, look at them as a reminder of how much you have achieved.
- Stay current with industry news. Doing so helps you be able to see trends in your industry and also gives you something to talk about at business events.
- Maintain your social media profiles. Every six months, update you profile. Make sure that your profiles and pictures are professional. Remember, employers, coworkers, current, and potential clients are looking at your profile to learn more about you.
- Have a professional photo taken for your social media profiles, email signatures, or even your resume.
- Take a business writing course.
- Be professional and timely in responding to business emails, and phone calls.
- Every quarter, set new goals for yourself.

- Ask for testimonials from your clients or professional contacts. This can be for your LinkedIn profile or to be kept in your professional file for future use.
- Keep letters, emails, and cards from clients, employers, or vendors praising you and your work. These will be invaluable for your annual review or if you are a business owner, for marketing purposes.
- Take initiative. If there is an opportunity to showcase your talents, do so.
- Change your mindset. Remember the Law of Attraction states that what we focus on the most is what we attract more of in our lives.
- Make Sundays your day of rest and relaxation.
- Avoid strenuous exercise just before the start of Monday and give yourself a little extra commuting time to avoid the stress of rushing to work.
- Move a big meeting to another day of the week, if you are in a position to control meeting times.
- Work from a place of passion. Find a job that matches your spirit.

Soul-Nourishing Food Six: Money

- Write down your beliefs around money. If they are negative thoughts rewrite them in the positive.
- Let go of your feeling of lack. If you continually worry about not having enough money, you will attract that energy.
- Look at your bank balances and feel a sense of gratitude for the amount you do have to pay the important bills.
- Check your credit report by going to www.annualcreditreport.com. This is the only site sanctioned by the government. You are allowed to get one report from each of the three reporting agencies each year.
- Set up a budget – make a list of your income and your expenses.
- Determine what expenses are needs and which expenses are wants.
- Make your envelopes for the different categories such as groceries, entertainment, dining out. Give one to each family member with an allotted amount of cash to be spent however they choose. Once the cash runs out, they will have to wait until the following month for the money to be replenished.
- Make a vision board of the life you imagine for yourself and for your family.
- Sign up at www.TastingWellness.com to be notified when our budgeting app becomes available.
- Write down what would be possible if you lived from a position from financial strength. Would it be volunteerism, reading, traveling, and helping family?
- Try to avoid using credit cards while living within your means.
- If your company offers a 401(k) plan with a company match, at minimum, contribute an amount up to the match. Remember, it is free money.

- Establish an emergency fund. Ideally, it should have enough money to cover 6-12 months of expenses should you not have work. At minimum, work to have at least a $2000 to cover the unforeseen expenses such as a leaky roof or a medical emergency.
- Establish funds for short and long term plans. A short term plan may be the purchase of a home or a car. A long term plan may be college, or retirement.
- Read your employee benefits book to know what is offered to you. Perhaps you get tuition reimbursement, or paid vacation. What happens to your income in the event of illness or disability?
- Negotiate the interest rate on your mortgage.
- Split your mortgage payment in two bi-weekly payments to save a significant amount of interest over the life of your loan.[75]
- Bring your lunch to work.
- Experiment with brewing coffee at home instead of purchasing coffee at a coffee house.
- Make a grocery list prior to going to the markets and avoid any impulse purchases.
- Visit consignment shops for clothing. Many have never worn clothing for sale at rock bottom prices.
- When shopping online, search for retailer coupon codes.
- Use coupons when shopping in stores. There are apps that have retailer coupons for in-store use.
- Omit services that are not being used such as premium cable channels or subscriptions to unread magazines. Little charges add up to big money over time.

Soul-Nourishing Food
Seven: Enlightenment

- Stay inquisitive about different topics.
- Learn a new language.
- Read a new book this week.
- Write a poem.
- Work a crossword puzzles and look up words that are not familiar.
- Help your children with their homework.
- Spend time in your local library.
- Listen to online videos on YouTube.
- Attend lectures and plays.
- Enroll in courses at your local adult education center, community college or other community group.
- Play games such as Scrabble, Trivia Pursuit, Sudoku, or chess.
- Go back to school.
- Play memory games like Mahjong.
- Practice daily memory exercises.
- Take a cooking class.
- Pick up photography.
- Learn how to play an instrument.

Soul-Nourishing Food Eight: Home

- Begin with setting a timer for 15 minutes and a space in your home. A lot can be done in 15 minutes such as putting in a load of laundry, putting away kids' toys, or unloading/loading dishwasher.
- Designate a room or space in your home for a small home office where you write your bills, keep your important documents, etc.
- Invest in a paper shredder to keep at home.
- As mail comes in, immediately discard all junk mail, and envelopes. Shred any credit card offers and documents containing personal information. Immediately file other invoices and documents away.
- Weather permitting, open windows to let in the fresh air.
- Bring fresh flowers or live plants into your home.
- Paint or decorate your walls. It can be just an accent wall or a whole room. Make a party out of it and invite friends and family to help.
- Clean windows.
- Change furnace filters. Mark on calendar to keep a record.
- Change out light bulbs to an energy efficient variety or full spectrum bulbs.
- Change batteries in smoke detectors.
- Install Carbon dioxide alarms.

Soul-Nourishing Food Nine: Creativity

- Brush teeth with different hand and in a different order.
- Dress yourself in a different order.
- Drive a different route to work.
- Set the table in an inviting fashion.
- Plate food in a creative way.
- Walk on the beach and pick up sea shells and sea glass that capture your eye.
- Hike and pick flowers, leaves, twigs. Examine their shapes, their markings, and inhale their scents.
- Doodle.
- Watch a play or musical.
- Play dress up.
- Make your Halloween costume.
- Sketch anything that strikes your fancy.
- Take a sewing class.
- Go to a poetry reading.
- Write an online review for a book you read or a movie you watched.
- Rearrange your furniture.
- Take pictures and play with the filters on the photo editing apps like the filters on Instagram.
- Place your photos in a photo album.
- Read a book to your children using different voices and faces.
- Take an acting class.
- See a comedy show.
- Go to a comedy improv class.
- Play hopscotch or a game from your childhood.
- Buy flowers and arrange them in a vase. Take in the flowers' scent.
- Send a nice or spicy text message to someone you care about.

- Change your morning beverage.
- Look online for images that resonate with you and post them on social media (make sure to include photo credits).
- Go to the museum and analyze at the paintings. Look at the brush strokes and the textures.
- When eating, see if you can identify the ingredients by taste.
- Walk outside without your cell phone and look at the details of your environment.
- Start a blog.

Soul-Nourishing Food Ten: Health

- Drink a cup or two of water upon waking and before each meal.
- Go into your cabinet and begin reading food labels. Notice how many products contain ingredients you don't recognize.
- Try a new fresh vegetable each week.
- Switch to organics slowly, if possible. Remember, start with the vegetables and fruits with thin skin.
- Be mindful of chewing food. Aim to chew each bite twenty-five times.
- Prepare extra food the night before to take for lunch the next day.
- Eat real food, not processed. Aim to shop the outer aisles of the supermarket.
- Switch your table salt to unrefined sea salt such as Pink Himalayan or sea salt. Table salt has been stripped of all its minerals using bleach and chemicals. Unrefined salt has 92 trace minerals and elements.
- Reduce your sugar intake. Little by little, swap out sugar by eating more sweet vegetables and whole fruit. Try sweet potatoes, carrots, berries, pineapple, or other fruits.
- Eat more good quality protein and fats if you are craving sugar.
- Choose whole grains instead of their refined counterparts. Instead of white rice which has been stripped of all its fiber and nutrients, opt for brown rice. Experiment with other options such as millet, amaranth, quinoa, or steel cut oats.
- Seek out the help of a certified health coach. Go to http://coaches.integrativenutrition.com/ to find one near you.
- Experiment with different eating plans to see which one works for you and is sustainable.
- Consult a naturopathic doctor.
- Schedule your annual physical to know your various levels such as cholesterol, hormones, etc.

Soul-Nourishing Food Eleven: Movement

- Begin your mornings with a glass or two of water to rehydrate your body and to ward off fatigue.
- Begin walking 15 minutes a day.
- Rent fitness DVDs online or from your local library. Find one that you enjoy.
- Enroll in a dance class.
- Play outdoors with your children.
- Walk the dog daily.
- Try yoga.
- Join a walking club if you enjoy group activities.
- Try one of the activities mentioned in Chapter 6: Movement.
- Book a vacation centered on activity such as a bicycle tour of a Hawaiian volcano or a walking tour in Italy.
- Join a fitness club.
- Hire a trainer for one or more private or group sessions.
- Try a pole dancing class for kicks.
- Do chair exercises at work. You can find many online.
- Get up from your desk every hour. Stretch and walk around for a couple of minutes to prevent your muscles from tightening up.

Soul-Nourishing Food
Twelve: Home Cuisine

- Go through your cooking tools to see what you have and what you need.
- Get rid of any cooking tools that are old, peeling, or unused
- Organize your kitchen to make it more efficient. For example, if you store pots and pans in your oven, find another place for them so the oven can be used more frequently.
- Go through your pantry and remove all products that contain high fructose corn syrup, dyes, and any ingredients you do not recognize or cannot pronounce.
- Look through cookbooks for meal ideas.
- Subscribe to cooking magazines. My favorites are Clean Eating, Vegetarian Times, Gluten Free, and Cooking Light.
- Take a cooking class if you are new to cooking or just want to improve your skills.

Soul-Nourishing Food Thirteen: Balancing Dual Energies

Feminine Energy:

- Take a dance class.
- Receive a compliment, support or a gift without self-criticism or reservation. When someone tells you how pretty or handsome you are, do not be self-deprecating. Instead, say, "Thank you!"
- Be giving of yourself.
- Be more in tune with your emotions.
- Be more communicative.
- Be supportive.
- Let your partner take the lead. If your partner wants to plan a trip for you both, allow him/her to do so without the constant need to take control.
- Engage in collaborative activities or projects -- such as a group class or a volunteer project in which you are part of a team.
- Laugh and live authentically.
- Separate from perfectionism.
- Let yourself be a little vulnerable with another person you care about.
- Find a hobby that is rooted in creativity -- such as painting, writing, music, photography, sculpting, etc.
- Practice Yoga.
- Practice patience.

Masculine Energy:

- Stop apologizing for everything.
- Ask for what you want and need.
- Give yourself the place you deserve in your home and in your family. (Don't be a mouse, be a lion.)
- Be more assertive.
- Ask for what you deserve at work.
- Ask for your raise without apologies.
- Be a leader.
- Test your entrepreneurial side.
- Try your hand at competitive sports.
- Be decisive and take action on a task you have been avoiding.
- Be direct in your communication. Get to the bottom line. As my father would say "Stop describing the cow and get to the point."
- Engage in activities such as weight lifting and running.
- Look people in the eye.
- Stand up tall and straight.
- Develop your self-confidence.
- Practice being still.
- Take on challenges.

PART III

Design Your Life
Blueprint

W hen you have something to work towards, life becomes more exciting, and less mundane. It is important to design your life so that you know how the outcome should look. Nothing is set in stone as life is constantly evolving. Goal setting is not about achieving perfection, but rather creating a blueprint for your life. Feel free to modify your goals as you move along. I recommend that you write down your goals on the following pages and every six months or so, see how things are progressing and modify anything, if needed. The act of writing goals is a powerful way to set your intentions in your subconscious. You may complete many of your goals without consciously thinking about them.

Let's begin with a letter to yourself listing all the great wins in your life and what you would like to happen for you within in the next week. Use an extra sheet of paper if needed.

Write down what you would like to accomplish within one month.

How would your life be different after six months? List what you would like to accomplish within that time period.

Imagine it is a year from now, what would you like to have accomplished and how would that change your life?

Think about your five year plan. Describe what your life looks like in five years. What would you like to see happen?

After 10 years? How has life changed? What would you like to see happen within 10 years?

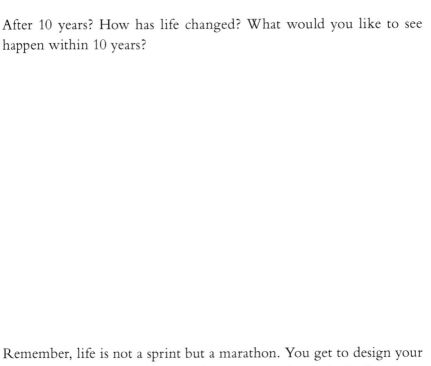

Remember, life is not a sprint but a marathon. You get to design your life any way you want. Look back at your entries periodically as you may be surprised by how much you have accomplished without even thinking.

Balanced Life
Happy **Life**

Journal

How to use this Journal

S oul-Nourishing Foods™ are areas of your life that feed your soul and make you feel happy and balanced. Those areas are: Socialization, Spirituality, Enlightenment, Money, Career, Home, Creativity, Self-Care/Inner Joy, Movement, Home Cuisine, and Relationships, Health, & Dual Energies. When one or more of these areas are not at the level you would like them to be, you have a sense of being off balanced. For example, perhaps your career is going well and you are just where you wanted to be as is your financial situation, but your relationships and home atmosphere are suffering or lacking. How does that make you feel? What small steps can you take towards bettering those areas? Would it be making time to date in order to find a life partner or scheduling a date night with your current partner? Perhaps it is hiring someone to mow your lawn as you dread walking up to your house because your lawn reminds you of the endless task of chores.

The key to finding a balance and joy in your life is to acknowledge the feelings you are experiencing in the moment. Give your emotions the attention and respect that they deserve. Most times, when you acknowledge and release these feelings, your mood will change considerably and allow you to make room in your life for the love, light and peace you long for.

I used to journal sporadically and only when sad or bad things were happening in my life. I've kept my journals from when I was a teenager and each journal was full of heartache or sadness. But over the last few years, I decided to use my journal on a daily basis for releasing all kinds of thoughts, and emotions. One of my nightly rituals is to pen all the wonderful, and perhaps not so wonderful, things that have happened to me that day no matter big or small. The act of journaling is therapeutic because you put your thoughts on paper and make space in your brain for new thoughts to come in. With us leading such hectic lives and with all the thoughts swirling in our brains, it is no wonder that we are stressed, tired, overwhelmed and have trouble getting a good night's sleep.

In the pages that follow, are a couple of weeks of daily pages for you to jot down what is going well in your life, what needs improvement, and what emotions you are feeling. Then end with a list of little things for which you are grateful. When you write down on paper gratitude for the little things, you start to realize that your life is full of little miracles and blessings. You can have gratitude for the beautiful loaf of bread you were able to bake or for the wonderful call you had with a friend. Take time to appreciate the little things in life each and every day. After a bit of time you will see your inner joy increase, and you will find more balance within yourself.

When thinking about your feelings, use S.O.U.L to help you pinpoint the emotion(s) you are experiencing in the moment. Remember, there is no wrong answer.

S.O.U.L. is an acronym for the following positive/negative feelings/ emotions:

Supported, **S**ad
Overjoyed, **O**verloaded
Upbeat, **U**nappreciated
Loved, **L**onely

Once you can better pinpoint the emotion you are experiencing, you can make better decisions on how to soothe or celebrate with yourself.

Sometimes these emotions are the cause for your spending habits. How we view and spend money has a direct correlation to how we feel about ourselves at certain times. It is with that thought that I included a place in your journal to record your spending habits, your current financial goals, and your financial dreams for the future. When we have a better idea of our spending habits and why we spend, we can make better informed choices that lead us on our path to financial freedom.

Week One, Day One

What am I feeling at this moment? Write down your S.O.U.L. feeling.

What areas of my Soul-Nourishing Foods™ are going right for me?

What are the Soul-Nourishing Foods™ I am deficient in?

What is one thing I will do today to enhance one of my Soul-Nourishing Foods™?

What 5 little things am I grateful for today.

1.

2.

3.

4.

5.

Week One, Day Two

What am I feeling at this moment? Write down your S.O.U.L. feeling.

What areas of my Soul-Nourishing Foods™ are going right for me?

What are the Soul-Nourishing Foods™ I am deficient in?

What is one thing I will do today to enhance one of my Soul-Nourishing Foods™?

What 5 little things am I grateful for today.

1.

2.

3.

4.

5.

Week One, Day Three

What am I feeling at this moment? Write down your S.O.U.L. feeling.

What areas of my Soul-Nourishing Foods™ are going right for me?

What are the Soul-Nourishing Foods™ I am deficient in?

What is one thing I will do today to enhance one of my Soul-Nourishing Foods™?

What 5 little things am I grateful for today.

1.

2.

3.

4.

5.

Week One, Day Four

What am I feeling at this moment? Write down your S.O.U.L. feeling.

What areas of my Soul-Nourishing Foods™ are going right for me?

What are the Soul-Nourishing Foods™ I am deficient in?

What is one thing I will do today to enhance one of my Soul-Nourishing Foods™?

What 5 little things am I grateful for today.

1.

2.

3.

4.

5.

Week One, Day Five

What am I feeling at this moment? Write down your S.O.U.L. feeling.

What areas of my Soul-Nourishing Foods™ are going right for me?

What are the Soul-Nourishing Foods™ I am deficient in?

What is one thing I will do today to enhance one of my Soul-Nourishing Foods™?

What 5 little things am I grateful for today.

    1.

    2.

    3.

    4.

    5.

Week One, Day Six

What am I feeling at this moment? Write down your S.O.U.L. feeling.

What areas of my Soul-Nourishing Foods™ are going right for me?

What are the Soul-Nourishing Foods™ I am deficient in?

What is one thing I will do today to enhance one of my Soul-Nourishing Foods™?

What 5 little things am I grateful for today.

1.

2.

3.

4.

5.

Week One, Day Seven

What am I feeling at this moment? Write down your S.O.U.L. feeling.

What areas of my Soul-Nourishing Foods™ are going right for me?

What are the Soul-Nourishing Foods™ I am deficient in?

What is one thing I will do today to enhance one of my Soul-Nourishing Foods™?

What 5 little things am I grateful for today.

1.

2.

3.

4.

5.

Week Two, Day One

What am I feeling at this moment? Write down your S.O.U.L. feeling.

What areas of my Soul-Nourishing Foods™ are going right for me?

What are the Soul-Nourishing Foods™ I am deficient in?

What is one thing I will do today to enhance one of my Soul-Nourishing Foods™?

What 5 little things am I grateful for today.

1.

2.

3.

4.

5.

Week Two, Day Two

What am I feeling at this moment? Write down your S.O.U.L. feeling.

What areas of my Soul-Nourishing Foods™ are going right for me?

What are the Soul-Nourishing Foods™ I am deficient in?

What is one thing I will do today to enhance one of my Soul-Nourishing Foods™?

What 5 little things am I grateful for today.

1.

2.

3.

4.

5.

Week Two, Day Three

What am I feeling at this moment? Write down your S.O.U.L. feeling.

What areas of my Soul-Nourishing Foods™ are going right for me?

What are the Soul-Nourishing Foods™ I am deficient in?

What is one thing I will do today to enhance one of my Soul-Nourishing Foods™?

What 5 little things am I grateful for today.

1.

2.

3.

4.

5.

Week Two, Day Four

What am I feeling at this moment? Write down your S.O.U.L. feeling.

What areas of my Soul-Nourishing Foods™ are going right for me?

What are the Soul-Nourishing Foods™ I am deficient in?

What is one thing I will do today to enhance one of my Soul-Nourishing Foods™?

What 5 little things am I grateful for today.

1.

2.

3.

4.

5.

Week Two, Day Five

What am I feeling at this moment? Write down your S.O.U.L. feeling.

What areas of my Soul-Nourishing Foods™ are going right for me?

What are the Soul-Nourishing Foods™ I am deficient in?

What is one thing I will do today to enhance one of my Soul-Nourishing Foods™?

What 5 little things am I grateful for today.

1.

2.

3.

4.

5.

Week Two, Day Six

What am I feeling at this moment? Write down your S.O.U.L. feeling.

What areas of my Soul-Nourishing Foods™ are going right for me?

What are the Soul-Nourishing Foods™ I am deficient in?

What is one thing I will do today to enhance one of my Soul-Nourishing Foods™?

What 5 little things am I grateful for today.

1.

2.

3.

4.

5.

Week Two, Day Seven

What am I feeling at this moment? Write down your S.O.U.L. feeling.

What areas of my Soul-Nourishing Foods™ are going right for me?

What are the Soul-Nourishing Foods™ I am deficient in?

What is one thing I will do today to enhance one of my Soul-Nourishing Foods™?

What 5 little things am I grateful for today.

1.

2.

3.

4.

5.

Balanced Life
Happy **Life**

Financial Freedom Journal

Sample Monthly Budget

Inflow

Monthly Income (All Sources)	_Amount_
W-2 Wages:	
1099 Income:	
Rental Income:	
Investments:	
Social Security:	
Alimony:	
Child Support:	
Total Monthly Income:	

Outflow

List all your expense in the table below. If an expense is paid annually, divide by 12 to get the monthly amount.

Monthly Expenses	*Amount*
Emergency Fund	
Federal Taxes (if self-employed)	
State Taxes (if self-employed)	
Retirement Contribution	
Mortgage/Rent	
Homeowner Maintenance Fee	
Utilities (Gas, Electric, Water)	
Internet	
Cable	
Home phone (Landline)	
Cell Phone(s)	
Landscaper	
Home Insurance	
Auto Insurance	
Life Insurance	
Health Insurance (if not offered through work)	
Individual Disability Insurance	
Long-Term Care Insurance	
Pet Insurance	
Clothing	
Tuition	
Groceries	
Food and Drink Purchased During Work Week	
Pet Food	
Mass Transit	
Savings	
Vacation Fund	
Long Term Goal Fund	
Prescriptions	

Doctor Visit Copays
Vet Visits
Credit Cards
Car Payment
Gasoline
Child Care
Personal care (Hair, Nails, Skincare)
Pet Care
Magazine Subscriptions
Miscellaneous

TOTAL MONTHLY EXPENSES:

The key with expenses is that they should be less than or equal to your income. If it exceeds your income, it may be time to re-evaluate your expenses for yourself and your family.

You will only experience the financial freedom you desire when you have your financial blueprint written down so that you know how to design your future.

Tools

If you like what you just read, you want to learn more about balancing your life, or you are looking for tools to make life easier...

Balanced Life Happy Life Bonus Content

Sign up to be on our mailing list at www.tastingwellness.com. We will notify you when our free bonus content is available. We are creating extra Soul-Nourishing Foods™ practice exercises, workouts, and more! It is our way of thanking you for purchasing this book.

Tasting Wellness Workshops/Teleseminars

Sign up at www.tastingwellness.com to be notified when the next workshop or teleseminar is scheduled.

Balanced Life Happy Life Journal

Love the journal pages in this book and wish you had a journal to record your thoughts? Sign up at www.tastingwellness.com to be notified when the three month journal will be available for purchase. It will include the Design Your Life Blueprint, the Journal, and the Financial Freedom Journal all in one complete journal!

Balanced Life Happy Life Journal App

Sign up at www.tastingwellness.com to be notified when our app will be available.

Tasting Wellness – Speaking Engagements

Book Elizabeth Gavino for your next live event! Call 201-659-7170 to contact for booking!

Tasting Wellness Private Coaching

Love the book but want individualized help in finding your joy and balanced life? Call 201-659-7170 or email info@tastingwellness.com to schedule your private coaching sessions with Elizabeth Gavino.

Elizabeth Gavino™ Collection

Elizabeth Gavino is working on a specialty clothing line that is sure to revolutionize your wardrobe! Sign up at www.tastingwellness.com to be notified when her clothing line is available.

Resources

Digital Branding & Content Strategy – Fable Collective (Owner, Noorindah Iskandar, created my book cover)
www.fable-collective.com

Editing Services – Colette Austin (my personal book editor)
racolette@aol.com

Therapy – Robin Kappy, LCSW
http://www.creativefocusing.com

Institute for Integrative Nutrition - Health Coaching Program (mention my name, Elizabeth Gavino, for a discount off your tuition!) or go to http://www.tastingwellness.com/become-a-certified-health-coach

No Milk Please and *No a la Leche* by Tatiana Barrera are available on Amazon.com or through her website www.naturaltatiana.com

Gluten Free Resources are available at www.tastingwellness.com

Naturopathic Medicine – Remede Naturopathics 646-485-5229 or www.remedenaturopathics.com

Follow Tasting Wellness on Facebook, Twitter, LinkedIn, Pinterest, and Instagram! Her articles are also on The Huffington Post www.huffingtonpost.com/elizabeth-gavino.

Bibliography

1   www.drnorthrup.com/blog/2013/01/hidden-emotions-hurt-the-heart
2   http://www.bloomberg.com/news/2013-11-22/harvard-yoga-scientists-find-proof-of-meditation-benefit.html
3   Huffington, Arianna, 2014, *Thrive*, page 131, New York, Harmony Books
4   http://www.eurekalert.org/pub releases/2009-10/osu-lan101509.php#
5   https://www.healthcare.gov/glossary/essential-health-benefits/
6   http://www.stress.org/emotional-and-social-support/
7   http://umm.edu/news-and-events/news-releases/2009/laughter-is-the-best-medicine-for-your-heart
8   What's a Normal Resting Heart Rate? http://www.mayoclinic.org/healthy-living/fitness/expert-answers/heart-rate/faq-20057979
9   http://www.psychologytoday.com/blog/dont-delay/201002/living-alone-can-canine-companionship-help-beat-loneliness
10 http://www.unh.edu/healthyunh/blogs/2013/01/11/CanineCure
11 http://www.psychologytoday.com/blog/made-each-other/201005/dog-good
12 http://www.aspca.org/fight-cruelty/puppy-mills
13 http://training.tonyrobbins.com/the-6-human-needs-why-we-do-what-we-do/
14 Comprehensive Psychology 2012, Volume 1, Issue 1
15 Behav Med. 2003 Fall;29(3):123-30.
16 http://www.cancer.org/treatment/treatmentsandsideeffects/treatmenttypes/placebo-effect
17 http://www.webmd.com/balance/features/transcendental-meditation
18 The Mysterious 'Medication' of Meditation http://www.webmd.com/balance/news/20000530/mysterious-medication-of-meditation
19 Northup, Christiane, MD, (2006) *Women's Bodies, Women's Wisdom* (Rev. ed.), New York, NY Bantam Dell p. 404
20 Northup, Christiane, MD, (2006) *Women's Bodies, Women's Wisdom* (Rev. ed.), New York, NY Bantam Dell pp. 135-136
21 http://www.nydailynews.com/news/national/70-u-s-workers-hate-job-poll-article-1.1381297
22 European Journal of Epidemiology May 2005 Volume 20, Issue 5, pp 395-399
23 http://circ.ahajournals.org/content/94/6/1346.full

24 http://www.drsinatra.com/heart-attack-risk-factors-rise-on-mondays

25 http://money .cnn.com/2013/08/12/pf/bad-credit/

26 Wilson RS, Mendes de Leon CF, Barnes LL, et al. Participation in Cognitively Stimulating Activities and Risk of Incident Alzheimer Disease. *JAMA.* 2002;287(6):742-748. doi:10.1001/jama.287.6.742.

27 McGraw Hill Higher Education - Discovery Channel. Neurons and How they Work.

28 http://karenhaller.co.uk/blog/branding-why-red-yellow-is-used-by-the-fast-food-industry/

29 http://healing.answers.com/spiritual-counseling/the-healing-benefits-of-color-therapy

30 http://www.lifestylefengshui.com/BaguaMap.pdf

31 https://www.youtube.com/watch?v=2bo lqFG 20#t=122

32 http://www.drnorthrup.com/blog/2012/11/shining-a-light-on-sad

33 BC Wolverton, WL Douglas, K Bounds (July 1989). A study of interior landscape plants for indoor air pollution abatement (Report). NASA. NASA-TM-108061

34 US Department of Health and Human Services. Public Health Service, National Toxicology Program. *Report on Carcinogens, Twelfth Edition.* 2011. Accessed at http://ntp.niehs.nih.gov/ntp/roc/twelfth/profiles/Benzene.pdf on October 9, 2013.

35 http://yosemite.epa.gov/opa/admpress.nsf/596e17d7cac720848525781f0043 629e/63605bd594c4aacb85257d020068a28b!OpenDocument

36 McCord CP. TOXICITY OF TRICHLOROETHYLENE. *JAMA.*1932;99(5):409. doi:10.1001/jama.1932.02740570055030

37 http://airnow.gov/index.cfm?action=aqibasics.aqi

38 http://www.ccohs.ca/oshanswers/chemicals/chem profiles/ammonia.html

39 http://www.musictherapy.org/about/musictherapy/

40 Am J Public Health. 2010 February; 100(2): 254–263.

41 White JM. Effects of relaxing music on cardiac autonomic balance and anxiety after acute myocardial infarction. Am J Crit Care 1999;8(4):220–230 [PubMed]

42 Cancer Nurs. 2005 Jul-Aug;28(4):301-9. Dance and movement program improves quality-of-life measures in breast cancer survivors. Sandel SL(1), Judge JO, Landry N, Faria L, Ouellette R, Majczak M.

43 The New England Journal of Medicine 2508 n engl j med 348;25 www.nejm.org june 19, 2003 Leisure Activities and the Risk of Dementia in the Elderly Joe Verghese, M.D., Richard B. Lipton, M.D., Mindy J. Katz, M.P.H., Charles B. Hall, Ph.D., Carol A. Derby, Ph.D., Gail Kuslansky, Ph.D., Anne F. Ambrose, M.D., Martin Sliwinski, Ph.D., and Herman Buschke, M.D.

44   Advances in Psychiatric Treatment, Emotional and physical health benefits of expressive writing, Karen A. Baikie and Kay Wilhelm, APT 2005, 11:338-346

45   Journal of Affective Disorders, Volume 136, Issue 3, February 2012, Pages 310–319

46   Paudyal P, Hine P, Theadom A, Apfelbacher CJ, Jones CJ, Yorke J, Hankins M, Smith HE. Written emotional disclosure for asthma. Cochrane Database of Systematic Reviews 2014, Issue 5. Art. No.: CD007676. DOI: 10.1002/14651858.CD007676.pub2.

47   Advances in Psychiatric Treatment (2005)11: 338-346doi: 10.1192/apt.11.5.338

48   Cameron, J. (1992)*The Artist's Way,* New York, NY, Jeremy P. Tarcher/Perigee Book, pp 9-11

49   Acad Med. 2010 Sep;85(9):1537-42. doi: 10.1097/ACM.0b013e3181eab71b. Nutrition education in U.S. medical schools: latest update of a national survey. Adams KM[1], Kohlmeier M, Zeisel SH.

50   Is Drug-Company Money Tainting Medical Education?; Kluger, Jeffrey; Time Magazine, March 6, 2009

51   Epidemiology of Celiac Disease: What Are the Prevalence, Incidence, and Progression of Celiac Disease?; Marian J. Rewers, M.D., Ph.D.

52   http://www.cureceliacdisease.org/wp-content/uploads/2011/09/CDCFactSheets10_SymptomList.pdf

53   http://www.forbes.com/sites/rosspomeroy/2014/05/06/are-you-really-gluten-intolerant-maybe-not/

54   http://www.naturopathic.org/content.asp?contentid=57

55   http://www.kaiserhealthnews.org/stories/2011/july/01/shift-limits-first-year-medical-students.aspx

56   http://www.webmd.com/balance/features/the-secret-and-surprising-power-of-naps

57   http://www.mindbodygreen.com/0-3423/What-You-Need-to-Know-About-Napping-Infographic.html

58   http://onlinelibrary.wiley.com/doi/10.1111/j.1530-0277.2010.01417.x/abstract

59   http://www.medscape.org/viewarticle/497982

60   http://www.forbes.com/sites/tanyamohn/2013/08/13/paid-time-off-forget-about-it-a-report-looks-at-how-the-u-s-compares-to-other-countries/

61   Vlahos, James "Is Sitting a Lethal Activity?" *New York Times*, April 14, 2011

62   ,[3] Amen, Daniel (2008) *Magnificent Mind at Any Age*, New York, NY, Harmony Books, pp 28-29

63

64 http://tuftsjournal.tufts.edu/2009/12 2/briefs/02/

65 http://www.csaceliacs.info/celiac disease defined.jsp

66 http://www.celiaccentral.org/riskfactors/

67 Libonati, CJ. Recognizing Celiac Disease. Fort Washington, PA: Gluten Free Works Publishing; 2007

68 *O'Bryan, Thomas. Blog Talk Radio Interview with Sean Croxton, Underground Wellness. Jul 07 2010. http://www.blogtalkradio.com/show.asp x?userurl=undergroundwellness&year=2010&month=07&day=08&url=glu ten-sensitivity-and-celiac-disease-with-dr-thom.*

69 http://www.epa.gov/pesticides/food/risks.htm

70 http://www.epa.gov/pesticides/food/pest.htm

71 http://news.nationalgeographic.com/news/2013/07/130718-organophosphates-pesticides-indian-food-poisoning/

72 *Radin, Dean et al. Effects of Intentionally Enhanced Chocolate on Mood, The Journal of Science and Healing, Volume 3, Issue 5, 485 - 492*

73 Journal of Nutrition Abstract April 1, 2005 Vol. 135 No. 4905-909

74 http://www.forbes.com/sites/nadiaarumugam/2012/01/26/how-size-and-color-of-plates-and-tablecloths-trick-us-into-eating-too-much/

75 http://financialplan.about.com/od/realestatemortgages/qt/Bi-Weekly-Mortgage.htm

Index

Printed in Great Britain
by Amazon